Peachtree Street,
Atlanta

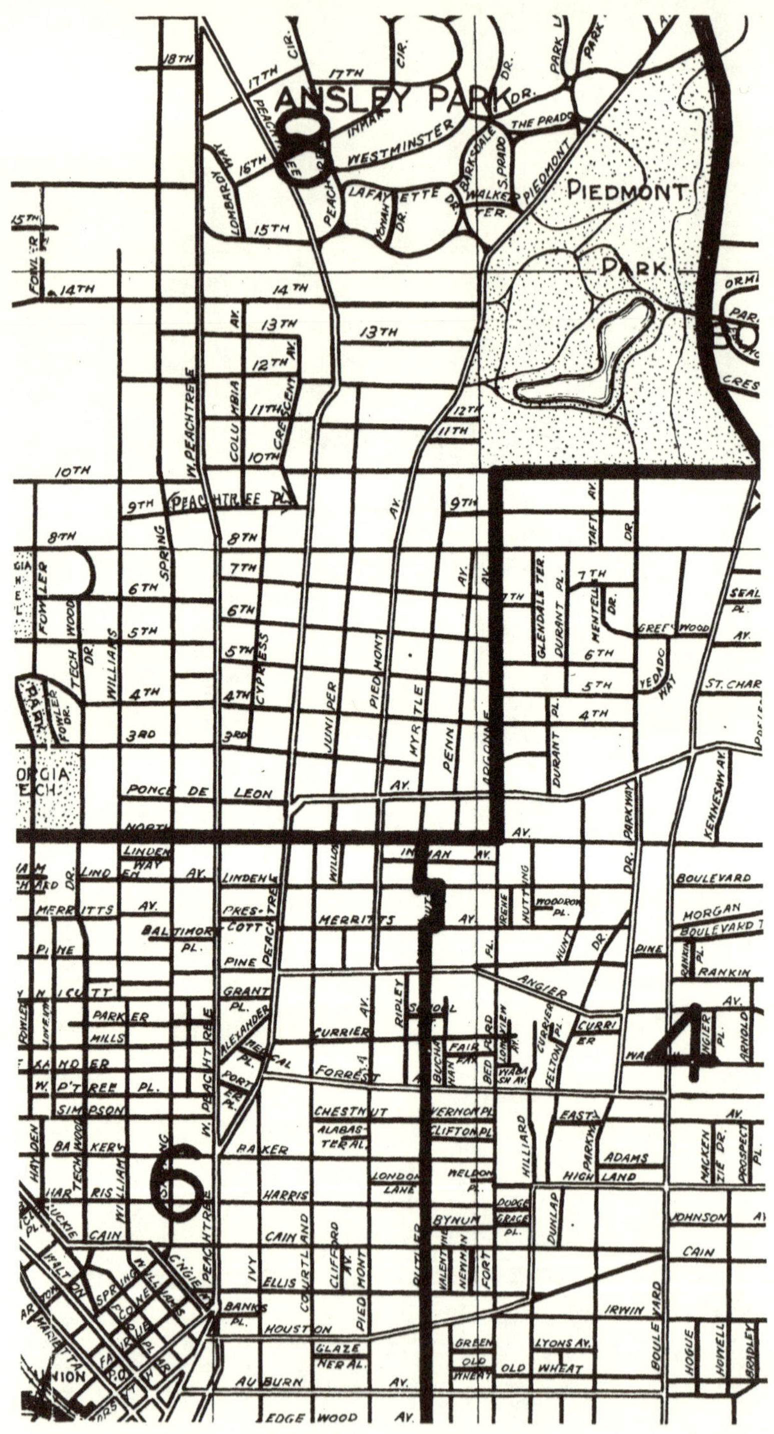

Peachtree Street, Atlanta

By

WILLIAM BAILEY WILLIFORD

UNIVERSITY OF GEORGIA PRESS
ATHENS

To
MRS. LUTHER WILLIFORD
whose tales of "old Atlanta"
inspired this story about
its best known street

Paperback edition published in 2010 by
The University of Georgia Press
Athens, Georgia 30602
www.ugapress.org

Printed digitally in the United States of America

The Library of Congress has cataloged the
hardcover edition of this book as follows:

Library of Congress Cataloging-in-Publication Data

Williford, William Bailey.
Peachtree Street, Atlanta.
176 p. : ill. ; 23 cm.
Bibliography: p. 169-170.
1. Atlanta (Ga.)—Streets—Peachtree Street. I. Title.
F294.A8 W65
975.8231 62-14238

Paperback ISBN-13: 978-0-8203-3477-6
ISBN-10: 0-8203-3477-4

Contents

	Prologue	ix
I	An Indian Trail	1
II	A Village Street	9
III	The Path of War	19
IV	Thoroughfare of Progress	28
V	A Street of Fashion	41
VI	Peachtree Kaleidoscope	69
VII	Music in the Street	83
VIII	Street of Many Mansions	93
IX	Violence and Visitors	105
X	Peachtree's Residential Twilight	120
XI	Up from Boarding House Row	137
XII	Pathway to the Future	162
	Notes	167
	Bibliography	169
	Index	171

Acknowledgements

THE author gratefully acknowledges the assistance which he has received from various persons and institutions while doing the research for this volume. Among these are Miss Ella May Thornton and the staff at the Georgia State Library; Mrs. Mary Givens Bryan and her staff at the Department of Archives and History; Colonel Allen P. Julian, U.S.A. (Ret.), and Mrs. T. J. Monroe of the Atlanta Historical Society; Mr. Stephens Mitchell; and the Reference staffs at the Atlanta Public Library and at the Ilah Dunlap Little Memorial Library at the University of Georgia. Special thanks go to Mr. Franklin M. Garrett for his personal assistance and for the invaluable aid received from his definitive *Atlanta and Environs*, and to Mrs. J. Thomas Bell, Jr., for typing the manuscript and making helpful suggestions about it. Finally, my appreciation must be expressed to Miss Ruth Blair who in her former capacity as executive secretary of the Atlanta Historical Society was most helpful in locating materials and in providing useful bits of information, and who since her retirement has continued to be interested in the manuscript and to dispense generous amounts of enthusiasm and encouragement.

Illustrations

Following page 22

Aaron Alexander Home — Wesley Chapel

Er Lawshe Home — Leyden House

James H. Porter Home — Five Points, 1864

Rhode Hill Home — Capital City Club and Richards-Abbott House

Following page 54

Henry Grady Hotel — Governor's Mansion

Federal Building — Dougherty-Hopkins House

Colonel Robert J. Lowery and His Famous Tallyho — Tompkins-Little House

Five Points, 1892 — Electric Building

Following page 70

John W. Grant Residence — Aragon Hotel

George Winship Residence — Howell House

First Baptist Church — Peters Residence

John S. Cohen Home — Fleming G. duBignon Residence

Following page 102

Georgian Terrace Hotel — Murphy Home
Men of Peachtree
Women of Peachtree
Rhodes Memorial Hall — S. M. Inman Home

Following page 134

Washington Seminary — McBurney Residence
Eugene M. Mitchell Home — First Presbyterian Church
Atlanta Historical Society — The Temple
Alcoa Building — Speer Mansion

Following page 150

Equal Suffrage Parade, 1913 — First Church of Christ, Scientist
Candler Building — World Premiere
Bank of Georgia — First National Bank
Retail Credit Company — Yesterday and Today

Prologue

A GENTLE snow was falling as the stranger walked slowly past the ornate bulk of a once elegant hotel. He puffed on his pipe and regarded the lines of automobiles and buses converging from five directions as an overcoated policeman blew shrilly on his whistle. The sidewalks were crowded with men and women loaded with packages, for it was Christmas Eve.

As he moved on, the stranger peered ahead at muted neon lights overhanging the sidewalks and at shadowy outlines of tall buildings with lighted windows glowing faintly in the grey afternoon. On he walked, past the shoe stores, the florist establishments, the candy shops, and the theaters. The notes of a beloved carol caught him up in a mist of memories as he passed a large department store. Pausing a moment to look in the window of a smart specialty shop, he wondered why it was considered appropriate for cruisewear to be on display over the Yule holidays and for Christmas items to have been exhibited since before Thanksgiving. As he turned away with a wry smile on his face, a street corner Santa Claus asked for a contribution to help some needy family.

The stranger's steps quickened as the snow stopped falling. Continuing past restaurants, book stores, and churches, he smiled appreciatively as the clouds parted and a ray of sunshine briefly illuminated the twin towers of an ornate apartment building. Still the traffic moved slowly past him; still the throngs hurried on with their tired and happy faces. At hand were the fashionable stores of the uptown district, and on his right was the aloof façade of a hostelry which had housed generations of dowagers and opera singers. It was here that he was staying.

Once in his room he looked from his windows and beheld the city spread below him. Then picking up the telephone and placing a long distance call he said, "Hello, Mary. I'm leaving by train tonight. . . . What?. . . . Oh, I'm in Atlanta–Atlanta, Georgia. And guess where I am at this moment. On Peachtree Street!"

Peachtree Street, Atlanta. What a variety of impressions it conjures up! To people all over the world it means lovely hoop-skirted women and beautiful ante-bellum mansions. To enterprising businessmen in the East it means a thoroughfare in a great and growing city. To people within hundreds of miles it means the fashion, cultural, and entertainment center of the Southeast. To long-time residents of Atlanta it means a bustling avenue lined with handsome buildings which have, regrettably, replaced the homes on the quiet, tree-shaded residential street of their youth.

Peachtree Street is all of these things–and more.

CHAPTER
ONE

An Indian Trail

THE origin of the street name *Peachtree* is obscured by the mists of time. Several theories have been advanced in an attempt to explain its derivation, but none of them is supported by documentary evidence. All are in accord, however, on one point: the name of Atlanta's most famous thoroughfare came from an Indian village which formerly stood near the city's present northwest boundary. Known as Standing Peachtree, it was located at the confluence of the Chattahoochee River and the stream which is now known as Peachtree Creek.

Standing Peachtree was the best known Indian settlement in the area. Easily accessible by land and by water, it was regarded by early settlers as a strategic point for travel and for trading with the Creek Nation of Indians. Even before the coming of the white man a network of trails led to Standing Peachtree. It was the terminus of the Peachtree Trail and the Stone Mountain Trail and was one of the objectives of the Sandtown Trail. The Peachtree Trail ran along the top of the Chattahoochee ridge from Toccoa in the mountains of northeast Georgia to Buckhead, a trading post established in 1840, which is today a fashionable residential area. At Buckhead the trail divided, one branch continuing west to Standing Peachtree and the other following Hog Mountain to a junction with the Sandtown Trail at what is now Five Points in the heart of Atlanta.

The earliest known written reference to Standing Peachtree is contained in a letter sent from Augusta by Colonel

John Martin (later governor of Georgia) on May 27, 1782. It states that the writer had been informed by the chief of the Tallassee Indians that a strong party of Cowetas had made plans to rendezvous at Standing Peachtree on May 26th, after which they would join a number of Cherokees and attack the Oconee Indians and the frontier settlements southwest of Augusta. Colonel Martin closed his letter with a plea for ". . . every and the most early assistance in your power—for God's sake exert yourself and come to our timely aid, as delays are dangerous. . . ."[1]

During the War of 1812 when many of the Creek Indians were aligned with the British, the State of Georgia made an effort to restrain them by erecting several forts at strategic sites within the Nation. One of these was Fort Peachtree, which was located at Standing Peachtree on a high hill just north of the mouth of Peachtree Creek, in the angle between the creek and the Chattahoochee River. It was a log structure, built late in 1813 by Lieutenant George R. Gilmer, who later became governor of Georgia.

Some of the early settlers of the area attributed the name of the Indian village to a giant pine tree, others to an unusually large peach tree. Exponents of the former theory said the name was derived from a tall pine tree on the hill where the fort was later located. The Indians were said to have blazed the trunk to obtain resin, or pitch. Hence this landmark was pointed out as the "pitch tree" and later the term was corrupted into "peachtree."

Proponents of the second version were convinced that Standing Peachtree's name resulted from a large and beautiful peach tree which grew on the future site of Fort Peachtree. Peach trees were not indigenous to the area, as were pines, but they could have been planted and cultivated by the Indians. Its location in the center of a clearing on top of a prominent hill would seem to lend credence to this theory.

The most authoritative word in support of the peach tree version came from George Washington Collier, one of the early settlers of the area and progenitor of a wealthy and useful Atlanta family. "Wash" Collier arrived in 1823 and settled on a vast acreage near Peachtree Creek. Years later, in recalling his early experiences as the carrier of the first mails between Decatur and Alatoona, he said, "Standing Peachtree post-office was right where Peachtree Creek runs into the Chattahoochee. . . . It was not Peachtree Creek then—they called it some Indian name. There was a great mound of earth heaped up there—big as this house, maybe bigger—and right on top of it grew a big peach tree. It bore fruit and was a useful and beautiful tree. But it was strange that it should grow up there on top of that mound, wasn't it? And so they called the post-office out there Standing Peachtree, and the creek they began to call Peachtree Creek. . . ."[2]

When Standing Peachtree was designated as a post office in 1825, it became the first town in the county to be so distinguished. Following the removal of the Creek Indians to the West a few years later, its importance rapidly diminished. Beginning in 1837 James Montgomery operated a ferry across the Chattahoochee at the site of the trading post, and shortly thereafter the name of Standing Peachtree was replaced on maps with the name of Montgomery's Ferry.

The extension of Peachtree Trail from Buckhead to its junction with the Sandtown Trail traversed the back of Hog Mountain. This range of hills was situated in an area of virgin forest abounding in wild game. The trail along the ridge of Hog Mountain was a main avenue for the canvas-covered wagons transporting intrepid settlers to the former Cherokee lands above the Chattahoochee River. It served also as a dusty route for lowing herds en route to the waters of blossom-shaded Peachtree Creek. The junction of the Peachtree and Sandtown trails occurred at a crossroads a short distance north of a settlement known as White Hall, which centered around a commodious two-story frame tavern of the same name. That portion of the Sandtown Trail between the tavern and the junction subsequently became known as Whitehall.

In 1835 Governor Wilson Lumpkin determined that Georgia should participate in a railroad building project, and late in 1836 the legislature authorized the construction of a railroad at state expense. In the following year Colonel Stephen Harriman Long, a career Army officer, was retained by the state for the purpose of making a survey and building the road. As a result of his efforts the legislature authorized the railroad to be constructed from the Etowah River south to Montgomery's Ferry at Standing Peachtree on the Chattahoochee River, and thence south ". . . to some point not exceeding eight miles, as shall be most eligible for running branch roads. . . ."[3]

The railroad terminal and junction point was located slightly to the west of the Peachtree-Sandtown intersection. Although sometimes referred to as White Hall or Thrasherville, it properly was known as Terminus until 1842. In that year it was named Marthasville in honor of Governor Lumpkin's youngest daughter.

In 1841 it was decided that the railroad should be extended to a point better suited for the erection of a depot and other buildings. Accordingly, the terminus was relocated in the next year at a site a hundred feet southeast of the Peachtree-Sandtown junction. Shortly thereafter the first lots in the new "town" were laid out and offered for sale.

With the completion of the state's Western and Atlantic Railroad from Chattanooga in 1842, the Georgia Railroad from Augusta in 1845, and the Central of Georgia Railroad from Macon and Savannah in 1846, the little settlement grew rapidly. The founding fathers decided that it needed a less provincial name, and so, on December 26, 1845, the legislature changed the name of Marthasville to Atlanta.

The first streets in Atlanta were Peachtree, which was the old Peachtree Trail; Whitehall, the old Sandtown Trail–a southerly continuation of Peachtree; Marietta, the old Indian trail to the town of that name; and Decatur, which was the eastern continuation of Marietta Street beyond Peachtree to the town of Decatur. These streets, and others soon to be laid out, developed in haphazard fashion. Early landowners doubted that Atlanta would ever be a real town; so they built upon their property as they saw fit. The result was crooked streets with houses and stores abutting at ungainly angles.

The original Peachtree Street extended only a few blocks north from its junction with Whitehall Street, after which it was known both as Peachtree Trail and as Peachtree Road. In the years ahead the Street would gradually encroach upon the Trail as the city grew and its residential district was extended northward. The main business area in the early days of Atlanta was centered around the section south of the Peachtree-Whitehall junction. The nicest residential streets were Whitehall and Marietta.

One of the first buildings on Peachtree Street was a simple one-story frame structure which Wash Collier erected at the northeast corner of Peachtree and Decatur streets. The property, extending back thirty-six feet along Decatur Street, was acquired by him on May 31, 1845, for the sum of $130. The store was built by the Peachtree Creek farmer to house his new retail grocery business, but following his appointment as postmaster it served also as the local post office. In an effort to clear his store of loungers awaiting the arrival of mail pouches, the brisk young businessman built along the Peachtree side of the store a porch upon which they could loiter, thus leaving the Decatur Street entrance free for the convenience of customers who might be inclined to spend a dollar or two on groceries.

One of the first houses built on what is now Peachtree Street was that of Patrick Connally, which was erected on the west side of the street on the first lot north of the railroad tracks. Originally Peachtree ended at its intersection with Marietta and Decatur streets, but in 1867 the name of the short block between that intersection and the railroad tracks was changed from Whitehall to Peachtree Street. Mr. Connally paid $400 for his one-acre tract in the latter part of 1845.

The lot adjoining the Connally property to the north was acquired by Jonathan Norcross on March 21, 1846, for $200. There, on the southwest corner at the intersection of Peachtree and Marietta streets, he built a store for the sale of general merchandise. The corner was thereafter known for many years as "Norcross' Corner." The man who gave his name to the site was a native of Maine who had moved to Marthasville in 1844 and established a sawmill in which he made crossties for the expanding Georgia Railroad.

In addition to the businesses operated by Collier and Norcross, there was a third store at the Peachtree-Marietta-Decatur intersection. Located on the northwest corner of Peachtree and Marietta streets, it was owned by Thomas Kile and was both a grocery store and a "drinking shop."

A few small stores were put up north of Kile's and Collier's stores, and several modest houses were erected beyond them. The town officially extended one mile in all directions from the railroad terminal (then known as the "car shed"), but it was several years before Peachtree was inhabited to that extent.

On the east side of Peachtree, in the triangle now formed by Peachtree, Pryor, and Houston streets, a non-denominational church and schoolhouse was erected early in 1847. The building, for which funds were raised by popular subscription, was of simple weatherboard construction with a chimney at each end. There being no resident preacher, services were held at irregular intervals. Atlanta's first Sunday school was organized there in June, 1847.

Several blocks north, near the edge of town, was located Atlanta's first public cemetery. Situated on the west side of Peachtree, it encompassed what is now the block between Harris and Baker streets and a portion of the next block to the north and extended west almost to the present Williams Street. The cemetery was laid out in the early days of Marthasville and soon became the repository for bodies of many pioneer settlers. An early resident, in recalling the first funeral she attended in the village, wrote:

"The first funeral I remember in Marthasville was that of a Mrs. Ball; she was carried on a wagon out Peachtree to a little graveyard near what is now Peachtree and Baker streets. Everyone walked and friendly hands performed all the last offices for her."[4]

Nearly a mile beyond the cemetery was located one of the first Peachtree residences, although it was not then within the town proper. The house was erected in 1844 for Alexander

F. Luckie, who had moved from near Covington in that year. Adjoining it was a small family graveyard in which Mr. Luckie and several members of his family were buried. The property was located at what is now the northwest corner of Peachtree and Prescott streets.

Atlanta of the eighteen-forties was a place of natural loveliness. As one pioneer settler recalled it many years later:

"I never saw more beauty than there was in the springtime in the groves all over Atlanta. All the undergrowth except the azaleas and dogwoods had been cut out. The sward was covered with the fairest woodland flowers, phlox, lilies, trillium, violets, pink roots, primroses—a fairer vision than any garden of exotics show now. Honeysuckles of every beautiful hue, deep red, pink, golden, white, were in lavish luxuriance. The white dogwood was everywhere; the red woodbine and now and then a yellow jasmine climbed on the trees. When a stream was found it was clear as crystal. I have seen few things in this world of [such] beauty, as were the Atlanta woods in 1848."[5]

A less poetic arrival of this period wrote in his journal:

"The woods all around are full of shanties, and the merchants live in them until they can find time to build. The streets are still full of stumps and roots; large chestnut and oak logs are scattered about,—but the streets are alive with people and the stores full of trade and bustle. . . . There are several beautiful springs in the village and the water is good;—the land is rolling. There are not 100 negroes in the place, and white men black their own shoes, and dust their own clothes, as independently as in the north. . . . The people here bow and shake hands with everybody they meet, as there are so many coming in all the time that they cannot remember with whom they are acquainted. . . ."[6]

The village grew at a steady pace. Newcomers were attracted by its climate, its strategic location on three railroads, and the opportunities they believed it afforded to enterprising merchants and artisans. Soon three newspapers were competing to bring the inhabitants news of their neighbors and of the great world beyond their ken. One of these, the *Miscellany*, printed a rhyme conveying some of the pride with which the village was regarded by its early residents:

> "Atlanta, the greatest spot in all the nation,
> The greatest place for legislation
> Or any other occupation—
> The very center of creation."[7]

CHAPTER TWO

A Village Street

As Atlanta grew, so too did Peachtree Street. The virgin forest through which it meandered resounded increasingly with the sharp blows of ax upon tree. The land was cleared, mighty trees were converted into lumber, and soon a dozen new houses lined the rutted red clay street.

The community's combination church and schoolhouse was engulfed by the northward spread of the residential area. By 1850 it was surrounded by simple frame houses and their companion stables and outhouses. By then, too, it was used for religious services by only one group, the Presbyterians.

In 1848 a small group of Methodists had built Wesley Chapel, a simple frame church located a few hundred feet south of the original structure. The interior was Spartan in its simplicity, with rough puncheon seats and a small table upon a platform which served as the pulpit. Illumination was provided by tallow candles set in wooden candle holders on the side walls and in a homemade tin chandelier hanging from the roof.

The first pastor of Wesley Chapel was the Reverend Anderson Ray, and his assistant was the Reverend Eustace W. Speer. When the Reverend William H. Evans arrived in 1852 and found no parsonage, he had one built on a lot adjoining the church to the north.

A few years later a bell was installed to call the faithful to services. Its sonorous tones were a source of annoyance to an invalid living on the west side of Peachtree Street; so her solicitous husband persuaded a group of mischievous boys to steal the clapper—which they did. It was not a part of the bargain, however, that the clapper should be deposited at the bottom of the new Baptist preacher's well—which it was. When the bell was found denominational harmony teetered precariously for several days, but it was restored by the Methodist preacher, who deprecated the incident and said he certainly did not think his good Baptist brother had filched the clapper.

Meanwhile, the Baptists, Episcopalians, and Roman Catholics had each built their own churches away from Peachtree and several years later the Presbyterians followed suit. It was to be many years before all of these religious groups would have churches on Atlanta's most famous thoroughfare.

While provision was being made for the spiritual needs of Atlanta's citizens, several schoolmasters had appeared upon the scene and forthwith set about educating the boys and girls of the village. Classes were held in the little community schoolhouse and at other locations.

Atlanta's first physician was Dr. Joshua Gilbert, a native of Clemson County, South Carolina, who had settled in Atlanta shortly after being graduated by the Augusta Medical College in 1845. His first wife was Elizabeth Humphries, daughter of the proprietor of White Hall Tavern. The good doctor regularly blew a whistle each time he reached a corner while en route to see patients, in this way letting citizens know that he would be out of his office and unable to see them at once.

A boardwalk was laid along a portion of Peachtree, thus affording protection against the red clay, which was alternately muddy and dusty. Along this walk moved businessmen en route to work, housewives bound for market, children headed for school, and whole families on the way to the village's first amusement park.

The park was situated between Peachtree Street and Walton Spring, the latter being located northeast of Luckie Street's terminus at Spring Street. Originally a wagon yard operated by a French émigré named Antonio Maquino, the park was conceived by him as a means of attracting customers to both the yard and the refreshment and souvenir stand which he maintained there. He contrived a giant wooden wheel patterned after contemporary mill wheels, and suspended between the two sections little cars made of wooden dry goods boxes. The wheel revolved on an axle and was rotated by two husky Negro men. This forerunner of the Ferris wheel provided many hours of pleasure for Atlanta's unsophisticated pioneers.

The future site of Peachtree's famous Five Points was, in the 'forties and early 'fifties, a muddy miasma in which cattle were not infrequently encountered. A pioneer resident of the period recalled many years later an amusing incident in which a sow was the central figure:

"In those days," wrote George W. Terry in 1909, "there was no law prohibiting live stock from running at large in the town, so old uncle Billy Mann had quite a bunch of hogs that ran at large on the streets and foraged where they might, and no one need say nay. Uncle Billy just fed his swine out in front of his store. . . .

"I was a boy clerk in Mr. Norcross' store at the time, and we boys and young men in the store used to keep a keg of ginger beer in the cellar with which to quench our thirst when we got dry, but sometimes it would get too strong or hard for a pleasant drink, and we would empty it out and . . . make a new brew. So one afternoon the keg was rolled out and the bung knocked out, and the fluid ran out into a little depression . . . in the hard clay, where it stood for a short time, till one of Uncle Billy's big, old longlegged sow hogs walked up and just swigged down a gallon or so of the stuff.

"She then started for her home up Whitehall Street, but she hadn't gone far before the draught in which she had indulged began to have its effect. She commenced to stagger and squeal, and finally went down the same as a drunk man would do, but her power of locomotion was gone. So she gently lay down . . . and slept off her drunk, just like many of our fellow men do every day of the year. . . ."[8]

When Jonathan Norcross was elected mayor in 1851 he defeated an opponent who had the support of the rowdy element of the town. After a few days in office the new official was called upon to try a tough member of this party who had been arrested after a street fight. When the accused was found guilty and fined, he pulled a long knife and attempted to reach the mayor. He was restrained, but that night his supporters stole from nearby Decatur a cannon which was a relic of the War of 1812. This they set up in the street and aimed at "Norcross' Corner." It was loaded only with sand and gravel, but repeated firings caused the courageous mayor's porch to look somewhat the worse for wear. Norcross stood his ground, however, and the rebels were routed after less than a day. Atlanta's hastily organized volunteer police department handled them easily.

The price of land in and near the village was astonishingly low. In 1851, for example, Nathan C. Carroll bought forty acres which included the present southwest corner at the Peachtree and Cain Street intersection. The price: one five-dollar pony. Some years later Mr. Carroll disposed of this property at a handsome profit by exchanging it for a pair of Indian ponies and a little surrey.

Atlanta's first large-scale landowner was Hardy Ivy, a South Carolina farmer who settled in the area in 1833. His log cabin, the first house in what is now downtown Atlanta, was erected at the present northeast corner of Courtland and Ellis streets. His farm extended on the north along a line from the present Baker Street to Forrest Avenue, on the east to the present Fort Street, on the south to the present Edgewood Avenue, and on the west along the present Peachtree and West Peachtree streets.

The owner of the largest parcel of land in the Atlanta of several decades later was Richard Peters, a native of Pennsylvania, who first appeared on the local scene as superintendent in charge of the Georgia Railroad's extension to what was then Terminus. Upon resigning in 1845, he operated a stage line from Madison to Montgomery. He became a permanent resident of Atlanta in the next year.

In 1856 Mr. Peters formed a company and built the largest flour mill in the Cotton States. To assure an adequate supply of firewood for the eighty-horsepower engines, he bought a four-hundred-acre tract of heavily timbered land on Peachtree Road. Then located about half a mile from town, the property extended on the north to what is now Eighth Street, on the east to the present Argonne Avenue, on the south to what is now North Avenue, and on the west to the present Plum Street and Atlantic Drive. The buyer paid five dollars an acre for property which was to enrich him and his descendants for more than a century to come.

The 1850's witnessed the construction of several noteworthy houses along Peachtree Street. One of these was constructed at the southwest corner of the Market (later Broad), Luckie, and Peachtree Street intersection, upon a lot which extended back to Wadley (later Forsyth) Street. The two-story structure, which was one of the first brick residences in Atlanta, was built in 1851 for Dr. Crawford W. Long, who later achieved fame as the first person to use anesthesia successfully in a surgical operation. After a residence of only one year the distinguished physician moved with his family to nearby Athens. The house was sold to Clark Howell, a native of Cabarrus County, North Carolina, who operated Howell's Mill north of Atlanta and who subsequently became a local merchant and judge of the Fulton Inferior Court.

The entire block across Luckie Street from the Long house was bought in 1854 by William Ezzard for $3,980. In the next year he erected a two-story brick residence near the Peachtree-Luckie intersection. It had a high front porch whose roof served as an upstairs balcony, and a small iron fence around the tiny front yard, both of which added a cosmopolitan air to lower Peachtree Street.

On the east side of Peachtree just north of the Church Street and Banks Place intersection, a house was constructed in 1852 for a newcomer by the name of Joseph Winship, who paid $580 for the one-acre property. Mr. Winship, a native of New Salem, Massachusetts, had moved to Georgia in 1820 and settled at Clinton in Jones County. Upon removing to Atlanta he established a freight car manufactory and the Winship Machine Works.

One of the most beautiful and famous houses ever built in Atlanta was constructed in 1859 or 1860 on the west side of Peachtree between Ellis and Cain streets. It was designed by John Boutell for one Henry Tarver, who appears never to have occupied it. Ownership passed almost immediately to William Herring, a prosperous clothing merchant. The house was box-shaped, having four rooms downstairs and four rooms upstairs, with a central hall running from front to back. The impressive façade was dominated by twelve magnificent Ionic columns, eight of which paraded their fluted beauty along the Peachtree Street frontage, while two more were visible on each side of the spacious piazza. Each column had a hidden opening at its base, presumably a hiding place for valuables. A small glass-enclosed observatory on the roof of the house provided a view of the entire town. At the rear of the structure were a brick smokehouse, a stable, and quarters for house slaves.

In the block beyond the Herring home, situated on the same side of the street and one lot north of Cain Street, was the home of Er Lawshé. Built in 1859, it was a two-story white frame structure with upstairs and downstairs porches across the middle of the front, and a high unbroken roof. A kitchen wing adjoined the house on the south side, and a white picket fence enclosed a large front yard. The owner, a native of Lewisburg, Pennsylvania, had moved to Atlanta in 1848 and opened a large jewelry business. Mr. Lawshé's unwavering integrity won for him the name "Old Reliable."

Er Lawshé's father-in-law, Willis Peck, built a house on the corner lot next to the Lawshé home shortly before the war began. Mr. Peck was a native of Raleigh, North Carolina, and was a plasterer by trade. He became wealthy in the post-war rebuilding of Atlanta and rose to a position of influence in his adopted city.

Across the street from the Lawshé house was the new home of Aaron Alexander. A narrow, two-story frame edifice, it had three upstairs front windows and two downstairs French windows which opened onto the front porch. Green slat blinds hung at all windows and a white picket fence enclosed the entire property.

Several blocks farther north was the home of Perino Brown, who had left his native Hall County to venture into Atlanta banking circles. Mr. Brown had recently purchased the small cottage from Washington J. Houston, for whom it had been built in 1851. Then located on the edge of town, it occupied what later became the northwest corner of Peachtree Street and Porter Place.

The addition of these and other houses improved the appearance of Peachtree Street and pointed to the role it would have later as an important residential street. In the years before the conflagration of 1864, however, the town's most fashionable residents were constructing imposing homes in the Washington Street area east of Whitehall Street.

As houses were erected for Atlanta's new residents, changes were being made in the appearance of downtown Peachtree Street, although business was still centered several blocks south on Whitehall Street. Wash Collier had demolished his small frame store at the northeast corner of Peachtree and Decatur streets and had erected in its place a three-story brick building. Among the tenants of this first of Atlanta's Collier buildings were *Medical and Literary Weekly*, Drs. Thomas and Taliaferro, editors and proprietors; Dr. W. H. Brown; Dr. M. H. Oliver; and Hunnicutt & Taylor. The latter firm, composed of James A. Taylor and Calvin W. Hunnicutt, occupied the first floor, where they had the town's most beautiful drugstore. The partners erected on the sidewalk in front of their business an iron column nine feet high which was surmounted by a highly gilded iron eagle with outstretched wings. This became their trademark and all of their advertising mentioned they were located "at the sign of the golden eagle."

On the east side of Peachtree, north of Collier's building and on what later became the northeast corner of Peachtree and a new street by the name of Cherokee (later Edgewood), there was erected a three-story red brick building which was named Cherokee Block. This edifice housed a number of businesses and organizations, including Odd Fellows Hall; Gate

City Guards; John H. Lovejoy, Wholesale Groceries & Liquors; F. A. Williams' Furniture; Manhattan Life Insurance Company; Dimick, Wilson & Co., Wholesale and Retail Dealers in Boots, Shoes, Findings, etc.; Georgia Air Line Rail Road; High, Butler & Co., Wholesale Grocers, Produce and Commission Merchants; and Lawrence, Campbell & McPherson, proprietors of the *Masonic Signet.*

North of Cherokee Block were some twenty brick business structures. Among the businesses and offices located between Cherokee and Houston streets were those of Richard S. Briggs' Family Grocery; Cox, Hill & Co. (William B. Cox, Rhode Hill, and William G. Herndon), wholesale and retail grocery; Boswell Y. Evans, grocer; Jeptha Robinson, wagon maker; and Chapman Powell, "German Physician." One or two private houses remained on the east side of Peachtree, while on the west side there were a goodly number of residences. From its intersection with Pryor Street near the home of Joseph Winship, Peachtree Street northward was devoted exclusively to residential purposes.

On the west corners of Five Points, which had come into being (but was not yet so designated) with the opening of Cherokee Street from Peachtree to Ivy Street, were situated the establishments of Jonathan Norcross and Thomas Kile. Above the latter's grocery store were the offices of Dr. Ezekiel N. Calhoun, physician, and Adam W. Jones and Samuel B. Hoyt, attorneys at law. Of these three men, Dr. Calhoun and Mr. Hoyt were to become especially noted for their contributions to the advancement of their adopted city. The former, a native of Abbeville District, South Carolina, had moved to Atlanta in 1854, while the latter had arrived in 1852 from his native Blount County, Tennessee.

Several important public buildings were located less than a block from Five Points. Among these were the Concert Hall Building, at the northwest corner of the railroad and Whitehall (later Peachtree) Street, and the Atheneum Building, Silvey & Glazner's Block, and Tanner's Block on the north side of Decatur between Peachtree and Pryor streets. At the northeast corner of Decatur and Pryor was located the new four-story Trout House, one of Atlanta's best hotels.

The Atheneum was a two-story building erected by James E. Williams, an East Tennessean who arrived in Atlanta in 1851. The builder's produce business occupied the first floor, and the second floor was devoted to a theater with a seating capacity of 800 persons. Here, beginning in 1855, Atlantians were entertained by Mr. and Mrs. William H. Crisp—"the South's most accomplished Shakespearean actors."

One of the largest crowds ever assembled in early Atlanta was enticed by an ambitious undertaking called "Fair of 1850." Conceived as an agricultural exhibit, it was held at a ten-acre site on a winding new road called Fair Street (now Memorial Drive). Peachtree Street and other thoroughfares were overrun with farmers and planters bent upon exhibiting cattle, porkers, agricultural products, and homemade furniture, while their wives sought to win blue ribbons for paintings, quilts, and preserves.

In 1854 Atlanta entertained for the first time a man who had been President of the United States. On May 2nd Millard Fillmore arrived from Augusta on a private car of the Georgia Railroad. He was royally welcomed by a delegation of leading citizens, driven over the thriving little city, and honored at an elegant dinner and ball.

The latter two affairs were held at the Atlanta Hotel, located at the southwest corner of Decatur and Pryor streets. Its proprietor was Dr. Joseph Thompson, a native of Spartanburg, South Carolina, who had moved to Atlanta shortly after the structure was built in 1846. The hotel's spacious grounds occupied an entire block, and Doctor Thompson's vegetable garden was long a familiar sight at what later became the southeast corner of Peachtree and Decatur streets.

On December 25, 1855, Atlanta was brilliantly illuminated when a new gas lighting system was turned on for the first time. The city had appropriated money for the purchase of stock in a new company which agreed to manufacture gas from Georgia, Alabama, and Tennessee coal. Fifty ornamental lamp posts were erected throughout the city, and soon the figure of the lamplighter was a familiar sight on Atlanta's streets.

A touch of color was added to Peachtree and its sister streets when Atlanta Fire Company No. 1 adopted a standard uniform. This volunteer group, the city's first fire organization, had been organized in 1851 with an authorized membership of thirty. Its uniform consisted of a red flannel shirt with black numeral "1" on front, black trousers, a fireman's hat with "Atlanta" and "1851" and "1" appearing in raised black letters on the front, and a black patent-leather belt with "Atlanta" embossed in the middle. Belts of the officers were white, as were the hats of the president and foreman. When the firemen went into operation, whether they were pulling the manually operated fire engine, unreeling its 500 feet of leather hose, or running a bucket brigade to a burning building, dozens of admirers followed their every move. Their motto, "Prompt to Action," and the dash with which they played their roles as saviors of the distressed lent an excitement to Peachtree Street such as it had never previously known.

Another colorful addition to the city was the Gate City Guard. Popularly known as the Old Guard, it was organized on January 8, 1858, in the Georgia Railroad and Banking Company's building on the east side of that portion of Whitehall which soon was to become the first block of Peachtree Street.

As recorded by historian Franklin M. Garrett in his monumental *Atlanta and Environs*, the membership of the Old Guard ". . . was representative of the best element of Atlanta's citizenship. The uniform of the company was a remarkably brilliant one, being dark blue, with dark epaulettes and trimmings, edged with gold. The hat was a black French shako, with drooping white plume. The service uniform was gray. The company, even in ante-bellum times, were well drilled, and noted for their proficiency in the manual of arms and company movements, and were the favorite corps of gala festivities. Three years after its organization the Guard was to have its mettle tested in mortal combat."[9]

CHAPTER
THREE

The Path of War

ATLANTA's forward march of progress and prosperity was stayed by the outbreak of the Civil War in 1861. Following Georgia's secession from the Union in January, the businessmen and residents of Peachtree Street immediately concentrated their energy and enthusiasm upon helping the South to emerge victorious.

On February 16th the present Five Points and the city park near the car shed were lined with several thousand cheering citizens intent upon welcoming the new President of the Confederate States of America. Jefferson Davis made a fervent speech in behalf of the new nation, as did Vice-President Alexander H. Stephens when he arrived on March 12th. Sandwiched between the two appearances was an elaborate ceremony held on the birthday of George Washington —he who had worked so tirelessly to nurture the Union which now his admirers sought to destroy.

Excitement swept the city early in April when the Gate City Guardsmen volunteered their services and left amid the boom of cannon and the cheers of their friends. On April 18th news of Virginia's secession reached the city and set off a tumultuous demonstration. The Atlanta Grays fired a salute of eight guns; church bells were rung; all business was suspended; and, as martial music filled the air, bonfires were lit on Peachtree and adjacent streets. The enthusiastic revelers were confident that the rising tide of Confederate unity was but a prelude to a glorious military victory.

Late in 1861 the Confederate government selected the lot at the southeast corner of Peachtree and Houston streets as the most central location to build an office for the Commissary Department. The property, which had formerly been owned by Wesley Chapel, had been deeded to the pastor in lieu of back pay. Shortly thereafter it was bought by Frank P. Rice, who agreed to let the government have the lot only if he was paid in gold. The commissioners negotiating with him offered payment in Confederate bonds, but Mr. Rice insisted upon gold, whereupon the government confiscated the property and erected upon it a two-story frame building. This edifice, the only building constructed in Atlanta by the Confederate government, was used for its intended purpose throughout the war.

On June 7, 1862, by which time Union forces had occupied several key Confederate cities, a strange procession rolled out Peachtree Street. The central figure was James J. Andrews, a thirty-three-year-old Kentuckian who had led a carefully chosen group of twenty-two Union men in one of the most exciting escapades of the war. They had stolen the railroad engine "General" near Marietta in an abortive attempt to sever the Western and Atlantic Railroad between Atlanta and Chattanooga. Pursued at a furious pace by the "General's" regular crew, which had commandeered a second engine—the "Texas," Andrews roared towards the Tennessee border as fast as the little engine could go. Finally, out of wood and water and unable to get up more steam, the "General" stalled two miles north of Ringgold. The pursuers aboard the "Texas" promptly captured most of the daring raiders. Convicted at a military court-martial held in Knoxville, Tennessee, Andrews and seven of his associates were sentenced to be hanged as spies. They were transported to Atlanta by train, arriving at the car shed early on the morning of June 7th. Andrews was taken immediately to the local military barracks in the three-story Concert Hall, which had been erected on the site of Patrick Connally's old home at the south end of Peachtree. After a short wait he was escorted to the street, where he entered a carriage drawn by two horses. Seated with him were Colonel Oliver H. Jones, provost marshal, and the Reverend W. J. Scott, pastor of Wesley Chapel.

With a file of guards marching at each side, the carriage moved quietly northward on Peachtree Street. Beyond Baker Street the procession continued out Old Peachtree (later West Peachtree) to Cedar (later Alexander) Street, where it turned right. Turning left at Peachtree, the party proceeded north until it reached a narrow country road (later North Avenue) and turned right. Continuing to travel in a northeasterly direction, the procession finally stopped at a scaffold which had been erected about a block east of Peachtree at what later became the intersection of Third and Juniper streets. There Raider Andrews was hanged. His body was buried under a nearby pine tree, where it remained until removed to the National Cemetery at Chattanooga some twenty-five years later.

Thus ended one of the thrilling personal adventures of what has been called "the last war between gentlemen." The two locomotives involved in Andrews' raid remain as vivid links to the long-dead past: the "Texas" is in Atlanta's famed Cyclorama and the "General" is in Chattanooga's Union Station.

The months following Andrews' execution brought many changes to Peachtree Street and to the populace of Atlanta. Martial law was declared in August, and in September the privilege of the writ of habeas corpus was suspended. The old city cemetery at Peachtree and Baker streets (from which all bodies had been removed prior to 1860 as the residential district pushed northward) became a military camp.

The gory Battle of Chickamauga sent hundreds of wounded soldiers to Atlanta, and the city's hospital and transportation facilities were sorely taxed. Businessmen of the city were requested to close their establishments at 4 P.M. and assist in caring for the wounded arriving at the car shed. Citizens were implored to send their carriages and servants both by night and by day to assist in removing the injured to hospitals scattered throughout the city.

Among the noted Atlanta houses which were fully or

partially converted to hospital uses was the columned mansion of William Herring. The aged owner's daughter, Mrs. Austin Leyden, presided over the Peachtree landmark both as family residence and as hospital until she and her small daughter refugeed to Athens. Her husband, a major in Longstreet's corps, was a native Pennsylvanian who had moved to Atlanta in 1848 and accumulated a fortune as proprietor of the town's first custom foundry and machine shop.

The Herring house, or Leyden house as it became known even before Mr. Herring's death in 1868, figured prominently in Atlanta's role in the great sectional conflict. In addition to being used as a hospital, it was the scene of considerable activity by the Confederate Signal Corps. This group spent much time in the observatory atop the house, from which vantage point a good view could be had of Federal forces on the surrounding hills. The observatory could be plainly seen by the Federal gunners, and they tried their marksmanship on it many times. None of the signal corpsmen were killed, but the big white house on the hill was a choice target. In the Battle of Atlanta a shell ripped through a left rear corner room and proceeded to the front room on the left, where it shattered a pier glass mirror and buried itself in a wall. Henry W. Grady, who later became a frequent visitor at the Leyden house, made a famous joke by opining that the shell "paused to reflect ere it ended its course."[10]

By consent of Mrs. Leyden, Lieutenant General John B. Hood, Commander of the Army of Tennessee, C.S.A., made the house his headquarters during the three battles immediately preceding the siege of Atlanta and during the siege itself. When Atlanta fell, General George H. Thomas, Commander of the Army of the Cumberland, U.S.A., who had been chosen by Sherman to garrison Atlanta, commandeered the house for his headquarters.

As Union forces advanced upon Atlanta, final preparations were hastily made for the defense of the city. The Peachtree defenses, consisting of redoubts, salients, and trenches, had originally extended from Merritts Avenue east of Piedmont Avenue to the present Peachtree-Ponce de Leon Avenue in-

AARON ALEXANDER HOME *Courtesy Atlanta Historical Society*
Built about 1850 next to northeast corner of Cain Street

WESLEY CHAPEL *Courtesy Mrs. H. H. Trotti*
Built in 1848, it was the first church in Atlanta

ER LAWSHÉ HOME *Courtesy Atlanta Historical Society*

Built in 1859 on west side of Peachtree, near Cain

LEYDEN HOUSE *Courtesy Atlanta Historical Society*

Used as Confederate lookout and as headquarters for General John B. Hood

JAMES H. PORTER HOME *Courtesy Atlanta Historical Society*

Scene of many brilliant social affairs in the 'eighties and 'nineties

FIVE POINTS, 1864 *Courtesy Atlanta Historical Society*

General Sherman's troops enter heart of city

RHODE HILL HOME *Courtesy Atlanta Historical Society*
Site of J. P. Allen Store

Courtesy Atlanta Historical Society
CAPITAL CITY CLUB (left) and RICHARDS-ABBOTT HOUSE, *circa* 1895
Site of Davison's Store

tersection, and on to the southwest section of the city. On July 18th and 19th these inner defense lines were extended so as to run from the Peachtree-Ponce de Leon redoubt almost due east to the North Avenue-Boulevard intersection, and from there to the southeast section of Atlanta.

The weeks preceding the entry of Federal troops were a time not only of military and physical preparations, but also of much religious activity. Revivals were held at several local churches, among the most successful of which was one sponsored by Wesley Chapel. The populace suddenly seemed to feel an urgent need for Divine communion.

Lieutenant General Leonidas K. Polk, commander of Polk's Corps, Army of Mississippi, C.S.A., and Episcopal Bishop of Louisiana, was killed in action at Pine Mountain on June 14th. His body was transported to Atlanta for a funeral service at the newly consecrated St. Luke's Episcopal Church on Walton Street. Later the cortège moved slowly from the church and proceeded to Peachtree Street and thence to the car shed; there the body was placed on a train for Augusta where it was to be entombed.

The Battle of Peachtree Creek, which began on July 20th, brought Union troops and artillery alarmingly close to Atlanta. The site of the initial assault was only six miles northwest of the inner defense line. With incredible rapidity the enemy dashed through the dense woods on Wash Collier's property and bore down upon the beleaguered little city. This one battle made old Peachtree Road a historian's happy hunting ground, but it claimed 1,710 Union and 4,796 Confederate casualties.

While the woods beyond Atlanta's northern boundaries resounded with the roar of deadly weapons and the cries of dying soldiers, Confederate General Hood made plans to attack the Union Army's General McPherson at his position in east Atlanta. Accordingly, at dusk on the 21st, segments of his army assembled on Peachtree Road at the site of the future Spring Street terminus. They marched up Peachtree to what is now Five Points and then moved out the old McDonough Road (Capitol Avenue).

While the battle raged, the residents of Peachtree—along with all other Atlantians—were helpless to avert disaster. The city was in turmoil as troops marched down and heavy army wagons rolled through its night-darkened streets. Federal forces commenced shelling the city on July 23rd, and Peachtree Street was filled with hundreds of terror-stricken men, women, and children. The tempo of bombardment was increased on August 9th; and thenceforth, day after weary day, the murderous rain continued to fall.

According to Wallace P. Reed, an Atlanta historian of the last century, "If any one day of the siege was worse than all the others, it was that red day in August when all the fires of hell, and all the thunders of the universe seemed to be blazing and roaring over Atlanta. It was about the middle of the month, and everything had been comparatively quiet for a few days, when one fine morning, about breakfast time, a big siege gun belched forth a sheet of flame with a sullen boom from a Federal battery on the north side of the city. The Confederates had an immense gun on Peachtree street, one so large and heavy that it had taken three days to drag it to its position. This monster engine of destruction lost no time in replying to its noisy challenger, and then the duel opened up all along the lines on the east, north and west. Ten Confederate and eleven Federal batteries took part in the engagement. On Peachtree, just where Kimball street [now Ponce de Leon Avenue, west] intersects, the big gun of the Confederacy put in its best work, but only to draw a hot fire from the enemy. Shot and shell rained in every direction. Great volumes of sulphurous smoke rolled over the town, trailing down to the ground, and through this stifling gloom the sun glared down like a great red eye peering through a bronze colored cloud. It was on this day of horrors that the destruction of human life was greatest among the citizens. . . .

"The vidette pit, out on Peachtree," Mr. Reed continued, "was one of the wonders of the siege. At this point the slaughter was so great that the pit was called the 'dead hole.' The pit was situated in front of the house of Mr. Columbus Pitts [northeast corner of Peachtree and Third streets. A tall pine in the yard was used as a Confederate lookout]. It was seven feet long, four feet wide and four feet deep, with a bank of red clay in front, and a plank step inside for the convenience of the videttes. Just opposite, at a distance of about a thousand yards, was a similar pit occupied by the Federals. . . . In [the Confederate] pit, from first to last, seventeen men were killed. They were picked off by the sharp-shooters in the Federal pit, and all were shot in the head as they exposed themselves to look out or take aim at the enemy. . . ."[11]

The Federal forces moved nearer to the heart of Atlanta as one smashing victory after another decimated, confused, and, finally, routed the Confederate legions. The city was evacuated by Confederate military forces on the night of September 1st, only to be entered immediately by riffraff, deserters, and Negroes anxious to taste their new freedom.

The city had not been formally surrendered by General Hood. On the 2nd, Mayor James M. Calhoun decided to handle that technicality himself in an effort to spare the city further destruction. He and several city councilmen and other prominent men discussed the situation while astride their horses at the intersection of Peachtree and Marietta streets. Included in the group were Julius Hayden, William Markham, Thomas Kile, Thomas G. W. Crusselle, and others. They set out, unarmed and carrying a white flag of surrender, to meet the Federal forces which were some two miles northwest of Five Points. After submitting a written request for protection for non-combatants and private property, Mayor Calhoun and his associates returned to Atlanta behind a contingent of Federal 20th Corps troops. The city's occupation was effected at approximately 11:00 in the morning.

On September 4th, three days before he personally arrived upon the scene, Major General William Tecumseh Sherman, commander of the Federal Military Division of the Mississippi, issued a special order which stated that Atlanta was required for military purposes and that all persons except the armies of the United States and civilians retained by them would leave the city at once. Sherman offered to provide transportation to points north or south and agreed to permit the evacuees to move trunks, furniture, and such servants as would voluntarily remain with their former owners. Union forces assisted in the evacuation of 446 Atlanta families, each of which was accompanied by an average of 1,654 pounds of personal belongings. Other thousands fled behind Confederate lines or to Nashville or Louisville.

Only a few hundred persons remained in Atlanta. They watched with dismay as Sherman's officers moved into the recently vacated residences of their relatives and friends. Several fine houses, including Judge John Erskine's handsome Peachtree residence, were torn down and the timber used in building cabins for the troops. The city was turned into a vast camp of 80,000 soldiers, who, after initially "requisitioning" whatever caught their fancy, surprised local residents by their restrained behavior.

Sherman began his infamous March to the Sea on November 16, 1864, leaving behind an Atlanta silent and empty under the pall of its still-smouldering ruins. The Union commanders had carefully destroyed almost every business edifice, mill, and railroad in the city, and a majority of its houses, although many of the handsomest residences were, unaccountably, spared.

General W. P. Howard of the State Militia wrote to Governor Joseph E. Brown one week after the departure of the Union forces: "Every species of machinery that was not destroyed by the fire was most ingeniously broken and made worthless in its original form. . . . Nothing escaped. . . . The enemy have destroyed from four to five thousand houses. Two-thirds of the shade trees in the Park and city, and of the timber in the suburbs have been destroyed. . . . All institutions of learning were destroyed. . . .

"There were about 250 wagons in the city on my arrival, loading with pilfered plunder; pianoes, mirrors, furniture of all kinds, iron, hides without number, and an incalculable amount of other things, very valuable at the present time. . . . Many of the finest houses, mysteriously left unburned, are filled with the finest furniture, carpets, pianoes, mirrors, etc., and occupied by parties who six months ago lived in humble style. About fifty families remained during the occupancy of the city by the enemy, and about the same number have returned since its abandonment. From two to three thousand dead carcasses of animals remain in the city limits. . . . The crowning act of all their wickedness and villainy was committed by our ungodly foe in removing the dead from the vaults in the cemetery, and robbing the coffins of the silver name plates and tippings, and depositing their own dead in the vaults. . . ."[12]

Wallace Reed described the devastation of Peachtree Street thus: "Peachtree street was burned up from the center of the city to Wesley Chapel. Hunnicutt's drug store was a heap of ruins, as was the commission house that stood beside it. Proceeding northward, where there had stood a number of buildings that were three stories high above the cellars [among which were Cherokee Block and several buildings owned by Joseph Winship], and in which most of the business of the city had been transacted before the war, there was nothing but a mass of ruins. . . . The mansions of Sasseen and Ezzard were left standing. Wesley Chapel remained, but it was horribly desecrated. Above Wesley Chapel, Peachtree Street had suffered but little. . . ."[13]

On July 7, 1865, Atlanta acquired a military governor in the person of Brigadier General Felix Salm-Salm, formerly of the 68th New York Regiment. A native of Westphalia, Prussia, he was a prince of the royal blood and a former Prussian cavalry officer who came to the United States at the outbreak of the war and was commissioned a colonel in the 8th New York Regiment.

Prince Salm-Salm's highspirited wife, the former Agnes LeClerq of Baltimore, shocked some persons by riding astride her mount, rather than side saddle, but her sympathy for Atlanta's war-ravaged populace melted her critics' disapproval. A highly cultivated woman, she was possessed of a graciousness which endeared her to a large segment of Atlanta society.

The Prince and his wife chose for their residence the home of Er Lawshé on the west side of Peachtree Street just north of Cain Street. There they entertained their neighbors and military associates at a series of friendly simple teas and dinners. The popular young couple departed Atlanta in October.

CHAPTER
FOUR

Thoroughfare of Progress

ATLANTA's first effort at resurgence was evident on May 21, 1866, when the doors of a new hotel were thrown open. This hostelry, the National Hotel, was located on the Peachtree Street property formerly occupied by the residence of Patrick Connally and his daughter, Mrs. Daniel Dougherty. Of red brick construction, the hotel had fifteen windows across the front of its second story. A third story was added *circa* 1872, and an ornate turret appeared on the southwest corner following a complete renovation and refurbishing in 1881.

Atlanta had been served by telegraph facilities since the late 1840's, but the office was situated on Peachtree Street for only a year or two following the war. In 1866 an office was opened on the second floor of the building occupied by Silvey & Dougherty on the former site of Wash Collier's Five Points store. It remained there until 1868, at which time it moved to the building which was used as the Capitol following the move of the state's executive and legislative offices from Milledgeville.

Silvey & Dougherty was a dry goods firm composed of two brothers-in-law, John Silvey and David H. Dougherty. The former, a native of Jackson County, had lived in Atlanta since 1847 except for two years spent panning for gold in California. He amassed a considerable fortune during the forty-odd years he was in business, and was an active and useful citizen in the realm of civic affairs. The building in which his business was housed was his personal property.

The name of Cherokee Street, a two-block street on the north side of Silvey's building, was changed to Line Street in 1866. It extended from Peachtree to Pryor Street and thence to the present intersection of Exchange Place and Ivy Street. At the same time, the city limits were extended on the north to what later became the intersection of Peachtree and Third streets.

On September 15, 1866, Peachtree Street and the houses and businesses lining it were illuminated by gas for the first time in almost two years. During the last six months of the war and the year and a half immediately following it, kerosene lamps had been used to illuminate stores, offices, and residences, while Atlanta's streets had remained dark. The restoration of gas facilities provided a major indication of the city's determination to recover from the horrors and inconveniences of war as soon as possible. Indeed, there was a prevailing sentiment that Atlanta should not only be rebuilt but should also become bigger and better than in the past—a "city" in every way.

The advent of freed slaves, carpetbaggers, and persons of doubtful character created numerous problems for the decent, hard-working, and law-abiding citizens of Atlanta. There was a sharp increase in the incidence of crimes of all types, particularly theft and burglary. Highwaymen even preyed upon travelers using Peachtree Road and other main arteries. On May 9, 1866, the *Atlanta Daily Intelligencer* reported that a government wagon was halted by bandits as it neared the intersection of Peachtree Road and Pine Street; the horses were stolen, and the unarmed driver was left with no clue to the identity of the malefactors.

Farther out Peachtree Road a shocking murder had taken place. John Plaster, a thirty-five-year-old member of a pioneer family of farmers in the area, was found dead after delivering a wagon load of firewood to customers in Atlanta. The site of the foul deed was a cluster of disreputable shanties lining both sides of the road at a place so narrow that it was known as "Tight Squeeze." In those days Peachtree Road between the present Peachtree Place and Eleventh Street wandered in a westerly direction along what is now Crescent Avenue. The heavily wooded area was separated from the later course of Peachtree Street by a thirty-foot ravine. As a result of Plaster's murder and other villainous crimes the grand jury recommended that a force of "secret detectives" be raised for the purpose of guarding approaches to the city. This resulted in improved conditions, and later "Tight Squeeze," desiring respectability, affected the name "Blooming Hill."

In 1867 the citizens of Atlanta seethed with fury over passage of the Reconstruction Act, which required that all eligible citizens be registered to vote, Negroes be admitted on the same basis as white persons, and delegates be elected to attend a convention at which a new constitution providing for Negro suffrage would be chosen. To top it all, military rule was resumed throughout the South.

The new commander of the Third Military District was Major General John Pope, West Pointer and hero of both the Mexican War and the Civil War. He arrived on March 31, 1867, and was escorted to the National Hotel, where he was elegantly entertained. A large group of citizens calling upon him were as surprised to see him discreetly attired in civilian clothing as he was to see them welcoming him. On April 12 he was honored at an elaborate dinner at the National. Following a concert by the 16th Regiment band many toasts were proposed, one of which was: "Our Pope—may he be as infallible as the law has made him powerful."[14]

For several years following the end of the war a controversy raged as to which of two streets north of Baker Street was properly the continuation of Peachtree Street. It was argued, with some logic, that the street which proceeded due north was really Peachtree. Opponents of this theory pointed out that the street which lazily wandered northeast had *always* been Peachtree Street. The rebuttal for this argument was that the latter was properly a continuation of Ivy Street.

There was a definite schism between residents of the two disputed thoroughfares. For a while it appeared that the due-north proponents had won, as the portion of the street to the east which extended north of Forrest Avenue was frequently referred to as Ivy Street. The two-block link between the Peachtree-Baker intersection and Ivy Street was called Oak Avenue. Later the controversial streets were known as East (or Old) Peachtree and West (or New) Peachtree, but the dispute continued. Finally, in desperation, the residents of West Peachtree obtained permission from the city council to call their street Georgia Avenue. This change was repealed in 1885 and from that time forward the two northern extensions of Atlanta's proudest boulevard have existed in resigned tolerance of each other.

The year 1868 was a momentous one for Georgia: following ratification of the Fourteenth Amendment to the Constitution of the United States the state was restored to the Union, military forces were withdrawn, a new state constitution was approved, and Atlanta became the new capital city.

On July 23 of that year a gigantic political rally was held in Atlanta in support of the recently announced Democratic candidates for President and Vice-President. Following speeches by Georgia's three greatest orators—Robert Toombs, Howell Cobb, and Benjamin H. Hill—a brilliant torch-light parade wended its way through the city. Peachtree Street, down which the bands and thousands of enthusiastic citizens from all over Georgia marched in clouds of red dust, was gaily decorated with bunting and flags.

The first post-bellum governor to be elected by the people was Rufus B. Bullock, a 33-year-old native New Yorker. Although technically not a carpetbagger (he had lived in Augusta before the war and had served in the Confederacy), he was, nonetheless, a Republican—thus suspect, and even hated. Bullock chose as his official residence the C. L. Larendon home on the east side of Peachtree between Baker and Ivy streets. This was one of several handsome structures which were occupied by newcomers destined to make their mark upon Atlanta.

The house at the northeast corner of Peachtree and Baker streets was the residence of William M. Lowry, who moved to Atlanta from Greenville, Tennessee, in 1865. Mr. Lowry was engaged in the wholesale grocery and banking businesses at first, but he soon concentrated solely upon the latter. He and his son and partner, Robert J. Lowry, early acquired a reputation for astute banking sense, and as a result rapidly became two of Atlanta's wealthiest men. The former was a progenitor of several families which to this day are among the most prominent and useful citizens of Atlanta.

On the opposite side of the street, directly across from the northern boundary of the Larendon property, was the home of William Markham. A native of Connecticut, he arrived in Atlanta late in 1852 and established a rolling mill. He had been strongly suspected of disloyalty to the Confederacy, but was permitted to retain his freedom throughout the war. His daughter Emma later became Mrs. Robert J. Lowry.

One of Peachtree Street's prominent and most promising men passed from the scene in 1869 when death claimed 37-year-old Colonel John W. Duncan. A native of Scotland, he was a lawyer, president of the Atlanta Gas Light Company, and had once been co-proprietor of the *Atlanta Daily Intelligencer*. He and his wife, the former Mary Fort of Milledgeville, lived in a charming cottage at the northwest corner of Peachtree and Harris streets.

An imposing two-story red brick house was erected in 1869 at the northeast corner of Peachtree and Ellis streets for Robert Flournoy Maddox. He was a native of Putnam County and had been reared in LaGrange, where his popularity and great physical strength had won him the office of sheriff at the age of twenty-one. Coming to Atlanta in 1858, he was a small merchant, until he left to serve with the Confederate States Army. Returning to Atlanta destitute after the war, he got a job clearing away the debris of the shattered city. After saving a small amount of money he entered the produce business; from 1869 to 1879 he had a tobacco and liquor store in the National Hotel; still later he went into the cotton and fertilizer business, and prospered prodigiously in both.

Mr. Maddox built his home on the site of a former home

of T. G. W. Crusselle. In later years he built a house on the adjoining lot for his daughter, Eula, and her husband, Henry S. Jackson—son of a justice of the Supreme Court of Georgia. The Maddox property was ornamented by a handsome wrought-iron fence.

In the same year in which the Maddox home was completed Peachtree Street acquired its costliest residence to date. The three-story brick structure was erected on a one-and-a-half-acre plot at the southwest corner of Peachtree and Cain streets. Its builder was John H. James, a 39-year-old native of Henry County, who had come to Atlanta in 1850 and subsequently made a fortune as a private banker. The ornate structure was generously endowed with balconies and dormer windows, and had a 60-foot tower. "Magnificent" brick stables, sweeping green lawns, sparkling fountains, and a large carriage house completed the extensive establishment. The frame cottage which had previously stood on the site was moved back to the Spring Street frontage for use as a servants' house. An iron fence surrounded the entire property.

On Christmas Eve, 1869, Mr. James threw open the doors of the "finest residence in Georgia." His hospitality was enjoyed by all classes of citizens, for while the owner did not move in the same social circle as some of his neighbors he was well acquainted with them in the realms of business and politics. A strapping, 200-pound "diamond in the rough," he was popular enough to run for governor at one time. His critics hooted, saying he was so unlettered that he spelled "dog" with two g's, but Henry W. Grady, editor of the *Atlanta Constitution*, squelched them by maintaining that "Colonel James is rich enough to squander an extra 'g' on a dog."[15] Perhaps this attitude was prevalent at the time of the housewarming, for in 1872 Mr. James was inaugurated as mayor of Atlanta.

Less than a year after the house was completed it was sold to the State of Georgia for use as the official residence of the governor, and the incumbent, Rufus B. Bullock, moved into the elaborately decorated house late in 1870. The sale price of the house and its furnishings was one hundred thousand dollars, which represented a profit to Banker James of a neat thirty-seven thousand dollars. It was generally agreed, however, that the state had acquired a real bargain.

The cornerstone of a new church was laid at the southeast corner of Peachtree and Houston streets on land adjacent to Wesley Chapel in an impressive ceremony on September 1, 1870. The congregation of Wesley Chapel formed the nucleus of the new First Methodist Episcopal Church, South. The aged timbers of Atlanta's oldest church building were soon hauled away. Shortly before the new church was completed, the steeple which surmounted the tower on the Houston Street side collapsed with a resounding roar. When finally the congregation moved into the 1,000-seat auditorium in 1878, an organ had replaced Wesley Chapel's melodeon, which had once been played by actress Fanny Kemble.

As Peachtree acquired attractive new structures an effort was made to improve the appearance of the street itself. The city fathers decreed that anyone who permitted "sweepings, paper, hair, food, slop or washings of any kind" to remain on Peachtree's street or sidewalks more than six hours after the marshal requested their removal, should be fined up to one hundred dollars or imprisoned for up to thirty days. In addition, all residents and businessmen on Peachtree Street were required to place refuse in a box or other receptacle outside their establishments on Tuesdays, Thursdays, and Saturdays so that it could be removed by the street overseer.[16]

Peachtree, along with all other Atlanta streets, was devoid of pavement, and only a few trees had survived the war to provide shade in hot weather. The street was a quagmire in winter and a rutted, dusty trail in summer. It was not uncommon for pedestrians and riders to be forced from street and sidewalks to make way for cattle, hogs, and mules being driven to market.

In 1871, Dr. John Stainback Wilson wrote in his book *Atlanta As It Is: Being A Sketch Of Its Early Settlers*, "The streets do not appear to be laid off with any regard to system or order. . . . The plan of the streets is about this:—*Where you find a road, take it.* . . . Peachtree and Whitehall are too narrow for the demands made on them. . . . Indications are favorable for the early completion of one or two important and much needed lines of street railroads. . . ."[17]

Atlanta acquired its first street railway system under the leadership of George W. Adair and Richard Peters in 1871, but it was not until August 8th of the following year that service was extended to Peachtree Street. The original route traversed by the Peachtree Street line was from Decatur Street north to Pine Street, but in 1874 the line was extended to Ponce de Leon Circle.

The first streetcars were pulled by two horses, but these animals were soon replaced by red-tail Mexican mules. The little cars, which accommodated sixteen passengers, had a driver's platform in front and a rear door and step for the use of passengers. Each car was equipped with a small glass-covered box into which passengers dropped their nickle fares. The driver had two bells, one for ringing up fares and the other for reminding forgetful passengers to pay.

The people of Peachtree Street soon became accustomed to the sight of the streetcars and to the sound of harness and fare bells jingling along the thoroughfare. Soon after these sounds were added, however, another familiar sound disappeared forever. With the creation of a full-time police force in 1873, the marshal no longer called the hours of the night as he made his rounds. It seemed strange at first not to hear the familiar "twelve o'clock and all's well" float over the silent city at midnight, but Atlantians philosophically accepted this as a part of the price of progress.

In the same year in which the police force was created, free mail delivery was inaugurated in Atlanta. On July 1, 1873, the first letter was delivered by carrier Charles V. Tutwiler to John C. Hallman, a partner in the wholesale grocery firm of Nunnally, Hallman & Company, at 55 Peachtree Street. Coincident with this service a standardized numbering system was begun for all houses and businesses. The Peachtree-Whitehall intersection was designated the center of the city, and the numbering of all streets emanated from that point.

An air of revelry pervaded Atlanta on January 6, 1873,

when the first in a series of annual carnivals was given by a group of prominent men who called themselves the Mystic Brotherhood. Patterned after the English Twelfth Night celebration, it included a parade, bonfires, fireworks, and a *bal masque* at the Kimball House. Peachtree and other principal streets were lined with thousands of revelers as "King Rex" majestically moved past in his chariot. The first Rex was said to be Logan E. Bleckley, later chief justice of the Supreme Court of Georgia.

As Atlanta slowly emerged from the crushing poverty which had gripped it in the first years following the Civil War, the city fathers, trying to keep abreast of the changes rapidly taking place on every hand, in 1875 pushed through a water works system. Firemen tested its effectiveness in a great display which attracted large groups of citizens to each street hydrant, the tallest of which—located on Peachtree Street near the residence of John H. James—threw a stream of water 143 feet into the air. With the advent of a water system better fire protection was afforded all citizens and the days of the home well were numbered.

One of the greatest improvements in the appearance of Atlanta's business district was made in 1877 when Thomas G. Healey erected a handsome three-story building at the northwest corner of Peachtree and Marietta streets. This edifice replaced the old brick structure which formerly had housed Thomas Kile's store. Healey had acquired the property late in 1876 for $11,500.

The progressive spirit which motivated Atlanta's resurgence from the ashes of war was clearly indicated by the inauguration of telephone service to 55 subscribers in 1879, when the invention was barely three years old. For the first two years of its existence the Atlanta Telephone Company occupied a room in the Kimball House, from whose windows the length and breadth of Peachtree were clearly visible.

Peachtree Street acquired several fine new residences during this period. A two-story brick home was erected for Nathaniel J. Hammond (later a congressman) on the west side of the street between Cain and Harris streets, adjoining on the south the home of Er Lawshé. A block north, between Harris and Baker streets, a handsome two-story red brick house was erected on the same side of the street for Captain James R. Wylie, a prominent banker and wholesale grocer who hailed from Chester, South Carolina. A narrow porch extended across the irregular front of the latter structure, and an intricate iron fence topped a stone wall enclosing the entire property.

Probably the finest home erected in this period was that of W. Rhode Hill, which was put up at the northeast corner of Peachtree and Cain streets. The owner was a poorly educated man from Campbellton who had been a railroad conductor and a whiskey salesman before acquiring a fortune as a wholesale whiskey dealer. He determined that nothing but the finest materials should go into his house, and so ordered the bricks from Baltimore. His wife, apparently a woman of charm and culture, installed a private theater on the top floor of the house. Many dignitaries were entertained in the spacious gas-lit rooms of the Hill residence and its owners were long famous for their hospitality.

Atlanta was host to two distinguished visitors in the late seventies, both of whom were honored at dinner parties. On September 22, 1877, President Rutherford B. Hayes arrived for a one-day visit undertaken to help establish cordial relations between the North and the South. After a parade through the city shortly before noon, the President and his party were escorted to the Markham House, William Markham's new hostelry, where President Hayes delivered a brief and cordial address. That evening he and Mrs. Hayes were honored by Governor and Mrs. Alfred H. Colquitt at an elaborate reception at the Executive Mansion. Mr. Hayes was an overnight guest at the mansion again in 1889, this time while traveling as a private citizen.

The second visitor of note was General William T. Sherman, who arrived in Atlanta on January 29, 1879, for a two-day visit. The occasion was not marred by any untoward incidents, although the General's visit of 1864 was still fresh in everyone's mind. It was suggested that Mayor James M. Calhoun, whose father had surrendered Atlanta to the Federal visitor fifteen years earlier, should offer the freedom of the city to General Sherman, but this plan was thwarted by an objector who said, "He made too damn free with it when he was here before." As Sherman's train rolled into the station a wag called out, "Ring the fire bells! The town will be gone in forty minutes!"[18]

After dining at the Kimball House, General Sherman and his party entered carriages for a leisurely drive along Peachtree Street and other thoroughfares which had known him in his more incendiary days. Next day the group was entertained at luncheon by Judge William B. Woods at his new residence at Peachtree and Kimball streets and at an informal reception at the Kimball House.

As 1880 arrived Atlanta was continuing to increase in size, and Peachtree Street began to assume greater importance as a fashionable residential street. A six-inch snowfall on December 29th, together with a temperature reading of two degrees below zero the following morning, clearly indicated that something must be done about the condition of the street. Efforts were made to improve the situation by filling the numerous mud holes which plagued vehicles and pedestrians alike and in 1882 a small portion of Peachtree was paved.

The heavy snow of 1880, which idled streetcars for most of four days, was not the only trouble which beset operators of the city's public transportation system. In that same year a number of citizens were amused by an incident which they witnessed one afternoon at the corner of Peachtree and Marietta streets. When the driver of a streetcar pulled by two mules of different sizes realized that his relief steeds were not present at the end of the line, he proceeded to change the mules from one end of the car to the other so that he could retrace his route on schedule. The mules, apparently realizing that their time was out and that injustice was being done to them, refused to budge. After several lashes from the driver's whip, the smaller of the two animals hesitantly began to move, whereupon the other mule took hold of her neck with his teeth and held her back. The driver became angry and continued lashing at them until the relief team arrived, fifteen minutes late, with the mules still stubbornly refusing to move. As the animals were unhitched to be returned to the stable, a Negro boy was heard to remark idly to a friend, "I always did 'spise a mule!"

Mules and horses were a common sight on Peachtree and other Atlanta streets, but nowhere were they more in evidence than at the wagon yards which dotted the city. Designed to accommodate the large numbers of farmers and artisans who brought their wares to sell to Atlantians, these picturesque yards consisted of large squares around which were stalls for the animals and second-floor quarters for the tradesmen. Three were located on Peachtree Street, the largest being John N. Wood's yard about three miles beyond the corporate limits on the north side of the city (at what later became Pershing Point). There, women in calico dresses and sunbonnets and men in rough homespun clothes, boots, and big straw hats sold the produce of their farms. Their laughter, fighting, and singing added to the colorful scene, and the noise fortunately was beyond the ears of the more sedate Peachtree residents.

As the town grew, Peachtree and adjacent streets were lengthened, widened, and otherwise improved. In 1880 the city fathers authorized the extension of West Peachtree Street from the corporate limits near the present Third Street northward to an intersection with Peachtree Road at Wood's wagon yard. In the following year the Fulton County commissioners authorized the chain gang to "proceed immediately to work Peachtree Street out to Mrs. Louise Werner's, that being the terminal point of the proposed alteration of Peachtree road, being a straight line from its intersection with the Plaster's Bridge road."[19]

The chain gang to which the commissioners referred was one of many such groups composed of convicted felons from the State Penitentiary. The State of Georgia, faced with a large influx of ex-slaves and criminals after the Civil War, was financially unable to provide an adequate penal system. It determined to lease the convicts to private individuals and companies, thereby relieving itself of the responsibility for their care. The system was inaugurated in 1868 and numerous fortunes were made through the use of cheap labor provided by these helpless convicts, for which the lessees annually paid the state an average of ten to twenty dollars each. Public indignation finally caused the leasing system to be ended forty-one years later.[20]

CHAPTER
FIVE

A Street of Fashion

IN the decade beginning in 1880 a large number of highly respected families were established in ornate new residences on tree-shaded Peachtree Street. Among these were several men who ventured into the virgin forest north of North Avenue (originally called Peters Street), which was known as Peters Park. This area was developed from the 400-acre tract which pioneer citizen Richard Peters had bought prior to the Civil War in order to have an adequate supply of wood for his flour mill.

In 1881 Mr. Peters moved his large family from their home at the corner of Mitchell and Forsyth streets to a two-story brick residence on the west side of Peachtree between Fourth and Fifth streets. The handsome structure had a commodious front porch extending across the front and south sides and was set back from the street in a bower of large oak trees. There Mrs. Peters, a daughter of old Dr. Joseph Thompson, reigned for many years as a gracious wife and mother.

The nearest neighbor to the Peters family was George Winship, who in 1880 had moved to the northwest corner of Peachtree and Third streets from his former residence on Ivy Street. Designed by the well-known architectural firm of Bruce & Morgan, his two-story house featured a steep roof and a wide veranda surmounted by iron grillwork. A beautiful sunken garden was for many years maintained between the house and Peachtree Street, and a wrought iron fence surrounded the entire property.

Mr. Winship was no newcomer to the fashionable thoroughfare, having lived for some years at the home of his father, Joseph Winship, between Houston and Ellis streets. A native of Jones County, he had served in the Civil War and had later become associated with the Winship Machine Works. He was one of Atlanta's first millionaires and was noted for his philanthropies, particularly to Emory College (now Emory University). First to preside over the Winship house was George Winship's second wife, the former Lula Lane of Macon. Following her death, he married Mrs. Elizabeth Thiot Bailey, a member of the Charlton and Thiot families of Savannah, who presided over the home until Mr. Winship's death twenty years later.

Directly opposite the Winship home, at the northeast corner of Peachtree and Third streets, was the two-story residence of Mr. and Mrs. Albert E. Thornton. Originally a small frame structure built by the Pitts family, it was greatly enlarged by Mr. Thornton after he acquired it in the early 1880's. The house was situated in the middle of a lot 200 feet by 400 feet, and large magnolia trees shielded it from the dust stirred up by horses and carriages on Peachtree. Four beautiful Tiffany stained-glass windows were features of this home.

Mr. Thornton, a native of Troup County, had lived for several years in LaGrange. Following his marriage to the wealthy Miss Leila Austell, daughter of pioneer Atlanta banker and capitalist Alfred Austell, he moved to Atlanta and soon became a vice-president of the Atlanta National Bank and president of cotton mills in Elberton and Milledgeville.

One block south of the Thornton residence, at the northeast corner of Peachtree and Ponce de Leon, was the home of Major and Mrs. Livingston Mims. The large two-story frame structure was set far back from the street in a grove of trees surrounded by a wide expanse of lawn. A brick walk stretched from the house to the street, at which point were located two large urns filled with flowers.

Major Mims was a native South Carolinian who had acquired wealth, a wife, and an extensive plantation in Mississippi, only to lose them all in the Civil War. After serving on General Joseph E. Johnston's staff during the war he became his partner in a Savannah insurance business. Soon, however, Major Mims moved to Atlanta and became southern manager for the New York Life Insurance Company. He and his second wife, the former Sue Harper of Brandon, Mississippi, quickly earned for themselves a place in the city's social life. Their charm and brilliance, combined with their gracious hospitality, made their home a gathering place for the cultured, distinguished, and interesting persons who lived or visited in Atlanta.

Across from the Mims residence, on the west side of Peachtree and adjoining the vacant lot at the northwest corner of Kimball Street (Ponce de Leon, west of Peachtree), was the home of Colonel Green J. Foreacre. When the owner moved to Ohio a few years later the property was acquired by Colonel Willis E. Ragan, head of the wholesale dry goods firm of Ragan, Malone & Company. Colonel Ragan, a native of Albany, Georgia, was an enthusiastic gardener and the flowers he grew on the corner lot were for many years one of the sights of Peachtree Street.

Around 1885 the lot at the southeast corner of Peachtree and Fourth streets, which adjoined the Thornton property, was acquired by Thomas M. Clarke. A two-story frame house was erected, and there a large family was reared. Mr. Clarke, a native of Augusta, was engaged in the hardware business in a store at the northeast corner of Peachtree Street and Edgewood Avenue. His wife was the former Joan Thompson, daughter of Dr. Joseph Thompson.

As the northernmost reaches of Peachtree developed into a fashionable residential neighborhood the blocks to the south continued to acquire new homes of similar grandeur. The building of residences even continued for some years in the area between the Methodist Church and Baker Street. Of the houses erected in the latter section, one was of particular interest to Atlantians because it marked a new high in local adaptations of ornate Victorian architecture. The three-story house, erected in 1884 upon a 59 by 275-foot lot on the west side of Peachtree between Ellis and Cain streets, was constructed of orange brick and terra cotta and was elaborately embellished with turrets, gargoyles, dormer windows, and porches.

The builder and first occupant was Robert H. Richards, wealthy banker and formerly a partner in Atlanta's first bookstore. A native of London, he arrived in the United States with his parents at the age of thirteen and settled at Penfield in Green County, Georgia. After living in Atlanta for a short time around 1848, he opened bookstores in LaGrange and in Knoxville, Tennessee. While living in the latter city during the war he invested heavily in various railroad stocks which later netted him a profit of a quarter of a million dollars. In 1865 he aided General Alfred Austell in organizing the Atlanta National Bank, of which he became a vice-president. His wife, a generous and hospitable woman, was the former Josephine Rankin of LaGrange.

Adjoining the Richards home to the south, at the northwest corner of Peachtree and Ellis streets, was the second home of the Capital City Club, which had been organized in the previous year. The incorporators of the club, most of whom later achieved distinction in the city's affairs, envisioned their organization as filling a need in Atlanta's social life, and their confidence was rewarded in the years ahead. The two-story structure was built of yellow brick with a spacious veranda extending across its entire front. Its builder was John H. James, who also had built the Executive Mansion at Peachtree and Cain streets, and the contractor was John Calvin Peck, a native of Sharon, Connecticut.

A view of the contemporary social scene was provided by the *Georgia Major*, a short-lived Atlanta newspaper, when it acidly commented on April 29, 1883:

"Atlanta has her dudes . . . among men in the trades and professions who have acquired fortunes, and know of no pleasure higher than a vulgar show of their purses. As a rule they are off-shoots of the most plebeian parentage and void of any of the virtues and refinements of persons of gentle birth and decent instincts. They are contributing to give Atlanta a reputation as a city of cod-fish aristocracy and shoddy society.

"Either a parvenu or a lucky adventurer, he attempts to ape the traditional bearing and customs of the *ancien régime* in the South, and, of course, makes a horrible butchery of the business. 'Dinners' are given with all the bizarre effects that a half dozen cookbooks and magazine *menus* can suggest; 'soirees' are held in which the recorded scenes of the salons of Paris, of Madame de Staël or George Eliot are sought to be duplicated, and are made ghastly and vapid failures; 'receptions' are held where the 'leather and prunella' of Vanderbiltism on a small scale offends the nostrils of true born people. Men of worth, ladies of intelligence and exalted refinement, by birth and education, are excluded from participation in such affairs, because they are poor and not able to 'reciprocate.' It is, of course, no hardship to such gentlemen and ladies to escape the disgust of such scenes, but it is legitimate that we should refer to them in order to establish our proposition, viz; that nowhere in America does the social 'dude' flourish more luxuriantly than in Atlanta.

"Ten years hence, when the society of this quick-growing and progressive city has been purged of its dross and been formulated into a system, there are scores of the high-toned 'dudes' of today whose liveried lackeys, cockaded coachmen and painted china, will have gone 'where the woodbine twineth,' and they themselves will be earning humble, and we trust honest livelihoods in the circles where they properly belong—and a long way down the social ladder from the top rung."[21]

Alas for the *Major* and its sympathizers, the parvenus were not to be so easily defeated. As the late Miss Mildred Cabaniss, long-time society editor of the *Atlanta Journal* and herself a debutante of 1889, commented shortly before her death, "When I was a girl I wasn't permitted to speak to some of these 'social lions,' and now they don't lower themselves to speak to me."[22] Miss Cabaniss and her circle seldom retreated; however, many of the *arrivés* of her old age would have been amused had they thought she was keeping them at arm's length.

The intersection of Peachtree and Marietta streets was the scene of a great conflagration in 1881 which brought a sense of loss to the sporting element of Atlanta. Soon after Captain James W. English was inaugurated as mayor he conducted a campaign against vice. The gambling paraphernalia collected in a series of raids was piled at the present Five Points and ignited, and the fire which ensued was large enough to be visible throughout most of Atlanta.

This intersection was the scene of other unusual activity three years later when a 2,044-foot artesian well was bored at its center. The water from the well was pumped by steam power and nearly 200,000 gallons daily flowed through the new pipes which had been laid under the principal streets. The entire cost of the well, including machinery, was about $50,000.

The artesian well was not the only improvement to come to Peachtree in 1885. Along with several other Atlanta streets, the thoroughfare acquired several blocks of pavement and sidewalks, the former consisting of roughly cut blocks of "Belgian" granite. Late in the year twenty-two electric lights replaced eighty-four gas lamps in the heart of the city.

One of the sights of Peachtree in this period was a paralyzed man who rode in a little wagon pulled by a goat named "Peter." Although named William Jasper Franklin, he was known by young and old alike simply as "the goat man." His livelihood was obtained principally by begging, but from time to time he sold peanuts or matches. Some Atlantians were not moved by the plight of the poor fellow, or perhaps not entertained by his comic behavior. At any rate City Council passed an ordinance which forbade him to visit the heart of the city. The goat man, however, chose to ignore this bit of meddlesomeness and continued to be regularly at his favorite stands at the Capital City Club and the artesian well.

The eighteen-eighties brought numerous distinguished visitors to Peachtree. A large group was attracted by the International Cotton Exposition which was held at Oglethorpe Park in an effort to promote the textile capability of the Southern states. A parade on downtown Peachtree and other streets signalled the gala opening on October 5, 1881. Led by the Gate City Guards and a military band, Governor Alfred H. Colquitt and a group of dignitaries rode in open carriages through the flag-bedecked streets. On Governor's Day, October 27, the Executive Mansion was the scene of an elaborate reception for the visitors. Later some two thousand persons were lavishly entertained in the mansions of such Peachtree residents as Mr. and Mrs. Rhode Hill, Mr. and Mrs. James H. Porter, Mr. and Mrs. Henry W. Grady, Mr. and Mrs. William A. Hemphill, and Mr. and Mrs. George Winship. The Exposition was a financial success and it focused national attention upon Atlanta as a manufacturing, distribution, and transportation center.

Atlanta acquired a new lawyer and Peachtree a new resident when young Woodrow Wilson hung up his shingle in a building at the southeast corner of Marietta and Forsyth streets. Recently graduated by the University of Virginia law school, he practiced in the Gate City for only one year, 1882-1883. During that time he lived at 344 Peachtree in the home of Mrs. J. Reid Boyleston, a young widow with an impeccable South Carolina background. The house was set back from the street in a grove of trees and was characterized by an air of leisure and generous hospitality. While spending two months in Rome on a legal matter in 1883, Wilson lost his heart to Ellen Louise Axson, who subsequently became his first wife. Thirty years after Woodrow Wilson departed the Peachtree scene for advanced study at Johns Hopkins University he was inaugurated President of the United States.

Among the Peachtree houses in which Wilson was welcomed was that of William Daniel Grant, which was situated at the southwest corner of Peachtree and Pine streets. It was a two-story brick structure with a veranda across a part of the lower front and was set well back from the street. A white marble nymph graced a fountain in the front yard.

The owner of the property was a native of Athens who

had been educated at the University of Georgia and who later served briefly as a Confederate army captain. Subsequently he was associated with his father in the railroad construction business. William D. Grant moved to Atlanta in 1871, and in the thirty years remaining to him he became the largest owner of real estate in Atlanta and one of the wealthiest men in Georgia. His library of expensively bound volumes, ranging from the Greek and Latin philosophers to the works of Charles Lamb, was one of the most complete in the Atlanta of that day.

Across the street from Mr. Grant's house was the residence of his parents, Mr. and Mrs. John Thomas Grant. His father, also a graduate of the University of Georgia, had retired to Atlanta in 1875 after serving as contractor on numerous railroad construction jobs throughout the South and was said to be Atlanta's first millionaire. His wife was the former Martha Cobb Jackson, granddaughter of Governor James Jackson and first cousin of Civil War leaders Howell Cobb and Thomas R. R. Cobb.

A block north of the Grant houses was the home of Henry Woodfin Grady, editor of the *Atlanta Constitution* and eloquent advocate of The New South. Mr. Grady lived in an attractive two-story house on the east side of Peachtree near the Merritts Avenue intersection. It had been erected in 1881 at a cost of $16,000. The second-floor guest room was decorated with amusing murals of "Uncle Remus" characters, those delightful creations of Mr. Grady's friend and co-worker, Joel Chandler Harris.

Henry W. Grady, a native of Athens and a graduate of the University of Georgia, had moved to Atlanta in 1872 as one-third owner of the *Atlanta Herald*. As a correspondent for various American newspapers between 1876 and 1880 he entered upon the great works of his life—creating better understanding between the North and the South and developing the agricultural and industrial resources of his region. After speaking on "The New South" before the New England Society of New York in 1886, he became a national figure overnight.

Grady habitually walked from home to his office in the *Constitution* building. One day, so the story goes, as he and a friend were strolling downtown, Grady doffed his hat and bowed toward a passing streetcar. The friend said with amused puzzlement that *he* had not seen anyone aboard who was known to him. The stocky editor replied that he hadn't either, "But I'm sure I must be known to at least one person on that streetcar."[23]

Grady's next-door neighbors were Mr. and Mrs. William Lawson Peel, who had moved to Atlanta a few years previously from the south Georgia town of Americus and quickly made a place for themselves in Atlanta's business and social circles. "Colonel" Peel, as he was usually called, had developed from an unschooled plowboy in his native Webster County to an official of the Maddox-Rucker Banking Company. His wife, the former Lucy Cook, was a graduate of Wesleyan College and was the daughter of Philip Cook, attorney, Confederate general, and Secretary of State for Georgia.

One of Atlanta's most prominent citizens lived in a house at the northwest corner of Howard (now Prescott) Street, half a block from the Peel residence. This was Walker Patterson Inman, a former resident of Dandridge, Tennessee, who had moved to Atlanta in 1859 at the age of twenty-nine. Through a forty-year association with S. M. Inman & Co., a cotton brokerage firm organized by his nephew of that name, Mr. Inman accumulated a considerable fortune. In his old age he acquired control of the *Atlanta Journal* and served as its president. His handsome Peachtree residence occupied the site which had once been the farm of pioneer citizen Alexander F. Luckie.

A newly rich wholesale dry goods merchant who moved to Peachtree in the 'eighties provided his more sophisticated neighbors with considerable mirth at the Piedmont Chautauqua in 1888. This undertaking, the brainchild of Henry W. Grady, was headed by Marion Columbus Kiser, a Campbell County farm boy who had had almost no schooling, but whose native industry and ability enabled him to build a successful business enterprise. One can imagine with what elation he eventually settled the second of his three wives and his children in a house on fashionable Peachtree Street, at the northeast corner of Forrest Avenue. As president of the Chautauqua, Mr. Kiser was scheduled to make a welcoming address at the formal opening ceremony. As he rose to do the honors, he fumbled in his pockets for the speech which Mr. Grady had written for him. Unable to find it, he looked at the assembled crowd uncertainly and said hesitantly, "Right down thar is whar I used to hunt foxes." Unable to think of anything else to say, he uneasily asked those closest to him, "Whar's Grady?" Next morning the *Constitution* stated that "President Kiser's speech was a model of good sense and good humor, well and briefly expressed. It was just such a sensible talk as was to be expected from so sensible a man."[24]

Atlanta and all of Georgia were saddened on August 16, 1882, by the death of Senator Benjamin Harvey Hill. The statesman died at his residence, 182 Peachtree Street, following a lingering illness. Peachtree and adjoining streets were draped in mourning colors for the Troup County farm boy who had been valedictorian of his class at the state university, a state legislator at 29, a member of the Secession Convention, a member of the Confederate Senate, a Representative in Congress, and, since 1877, a United States Senator.

The funeral was held at the First Methodist Church, southeast corner of Peachtree and Houston streets, on the afternoon of August 19. Prominent men from throughout the South joined a group of Atlanta's leading citizens in serving as ushers, aides, pallbearers, and honor escort at the rites. Captain James W. English, Mayor of Atlanta, served as marshal for the occasion. The procession from the church to the cemetery consisted of hundreds of official mourners on foot, followed by some fifty horse-drawn carriages. The late senator's residence on the west side of Peachtree just north of Harris Street was surrounded by a large group of people long before the cortège left for the church. The *Atlanta Constitution* estimated that twenty thousand grieving or curious persons lined the route from the residence to the church and from the church to Oakland Cemetery. The newspaper went on to state with awed pride that Senator Hill's pure bronze casket cost one thousand dollars and that it was an exact replica of the one in which President James A. Garfield had been buried.

Four years later Peachtree was again the scene of a tribute to Benjamin Harvey Hill when on May 1, 1886, an Italian marble statue of the statesman was unveiled at the southern intersection of Peachtree and West Peachtree streets.

While the occasion honored the memory of Senator Hill, it developed into a magnificent personal triumph for the honor guest of the day, former Confederate President Jefferson Davis. Arriving by train from his home in Mississippi, the aged warrior was placed in a carriage whose wheels had been gaily decorated with red, white, and blue streamers. As the vehicle rolled out Peachtree to the residence of Senator Hill's widow, where Mr. Davis was a guest on the nights before and after the unveiling, six thousand school children tossed flowers into the body of the carriage.

The ceremony itself was dramatic. The eloquent Henry W. Grady was master of ceremonies; General Clement A. Evans, the lawyer-soldier-preacher who had conducted Hill's funeral, delivered a moving invocation; Dr. R. D. Spalding presented the statue to Governor Henry D. McDaniel, who accepted it for the State of Georgia; Major J. C. C. Black of Augusta delivered an address on the life and character of Senator Hill.

While Major Black was speaking a solitary horseman rode slowly and majestically down Peachtree. As he drew closer the rider was seen to be General James Longstreet, attired in the full dress uniform of a Confederate lieutenant general. As he approached the platform and deliberately mounted its steps the crowd of spectators, who were aware of the coolness between Longstreet and Davis after the war, watched in hushed expectation. Slowly the feeble one-time President of the Confederate States of America rose to his feet and advanced to meet his former associate; as they embraced with visible emotion a great cheer rose from ten thousand Confederate veterans.

The high point of the festivities came a few minutes later when Mr. Grady, in formally introducing Mr. Davis, said, "My countrymen, let us teach the lesson in this old man's life, that defeat has its glories no less than victory. . . . Rise and give your hearts to him as we tell Jefferson Davis that he is at home among his people."[25] A roar of applause broke forth from a hundred thousand throats as the frail, white-haired old gentleman rose and bowed. He delivered a brief speech and as he concluded there was scarcely a dry eye in the audience. So ended a memorable day in the history of Atlanta.

The monument to Benjamin Harvey Hill occupied a commanding position at Peachtree's most populous intersection. To the rear of the monument, in the triangle formed by the two Peachtrees, was the residence of Clarence Knowles, an insurance man who later became the first president of the Piedmont Driving Club. The house was built, *circa* 1869, for Hannibal Ingalls Kimball, who lived in it until 1875.

Mr. Kimball was a flamboyant entrepreneur who twice cast his fortunes with Atlanta. A native of Maine, he acquired wealth as a partner with George M. Pullman in the sleeping car business. While visiting in Atlanta in 1866, when he was thirty-four years old, he visualized the opportunities awaiting men of enterprise, and shortly thereafter he moved to the struggling, war-devastated town. As someone later wrote of him, "He was generous, bold, dashing and gifted with extraordinary magnetism. He burst at once upon the public view of Atlanta and blazed like a comet for more than 15 years. It was not long before he had his hand in more public enterprises than any other half dozen men in Georgia."[26]

It was not long, either, before the remarkable Mr. Kimball was accused of having sticky fingers on that versatile hand. His difficulty arose from a scandal revolving around the Opera House, at the southwest corner of Marietta and Forsyth streets, which the state legislature had decided to lease for use as a Capitol. (The old building on Washington Street, which the state had shared with Atlanta and Fulton County since removal of the capital from Milledgeville in 1868, had long since become inadequate.) In 1869 H. I. Kimball bought the property from his brother, E. N. Kimball, for a nominal sum and one year later sold it to the state for $250,000 in state bonds. In making the transfer Kimball failed to mention that a $60,000 mortgage was outstanding. Previously he had inspired considerable wrath when he persuaded his cohort, Governor Rufus B. Bullock, to advance $54,000 in state funds for furnishing the new executive and legislative quarters.

The political manipulations and financial double-dealing of Bullock and Kimball over a period of years involved them in unnumbered controversies and earned them the hatred of a large number of Atlanta's citizens. Whereas the New York-born Bullock is more or less forgotten today, his Yankee neighbor and long-time Atlanta associate has been remembered into the second half of the twentieth century.

Kimball's greatest local fame, and certainly his most worthwhile contribution to his adopted city, derives from a duo of hotels which he built on the site of old Dr. Joseph Thompson's ante-bellum Atlanta Hotel. Both were called the Kimball House and both in their day were the center of political, business, and social gatherings which affected the course of local, state, and sometimes national affairs. The first hotel was a six-story structure, which at its opening in 1870 was the largest hotel in the South. It was the first building in Atlanta to have a central heating plant and safety passenger elevators. This "luxurious, splendid, palatial" hostelry was destroyed by fire in 1883.

Kimball, who had left Georgia several years earlier "for reasons of health," hurried back to Atlanta and set about building an even grander hotel. The seven-story brick Dutch Renaissance structure was completed in 1884 and for thirty years was the scene of glittering balls and elegant dinner parties, political plotting, financial "dealing," and reunions of ante-bellum leaders. In 1902 ownership was acquired by financier Hugh T. Inman, who made a gift of it to his son-in-law, John W. Grant. The grandeur of the Kimball House faded gradually with time and it became just another begrimed, third-rate hotel, but Atlantians still regarded it with a peculiar affection and its bulk continued to dominate the first block of Peachtree Street until it was demolished in 1959.

The towers and turrets of the Kimball House were not the only additions to the Five Points area in the 1880's. Thomas M. Clarke's hardware business acquired new competition when George E. King, a frail South Carolinian, opened a hardware store at the southeast corner of Peachtree and Wheat Street (now Auburn Avenue). The business thus started in a small way ultimately became King Hardware Company, which flourishes today with a variety of strategically located outlets. As he prospered George King acquired ownership of the Clarke firm and of Hunnicutt & Bellingrath, which had been in business at the northwest corner of Peachtree and Walton streets since 1872.

Calvin W. Hunnicutt, co-owner of Hunnicutt & Bellingrath, was a North Carolinian who had moved to Atlanta in 1852. His first business enterprise was a retail dry goods store which he opened in partnership with John Silvey. Both men acquired considerable wealth in later years after their paths diverged.

An enterprising young druggist created a sensation in 1885 when he introduced the penny to retail trade. Dr. Joseph Jacobs, who in his youth had been apprenticed to Dr. Crawford W. Long in his home town of Jefferson, had bought a drug business in the Norcross Building at the southwest corner of Peachtree and Marietta streets. To boost sales he ordered 3,000 pennies and advertised items for sale at such unheard-of prices as 17¢, 29¢, and 98¢. Until that time the nickel had been the smallest medium of local exchange and prices had been set in sensible round figures. As customers flocked to his counters Dr. Jacobs was threatened with lawsuits and even physical violence, but in time the indignation of other merchants subsided. A new retail merchandising concept had been born.

Jacobs' Drug Store became an important member of the Atlanta business community and ultimately there were several Jacobs drug stores on Peachtree and other streets. The original store's greatest claim to fame, however, came in 1887 when the operator of the soda fountain inadvertently served the first

HENRY GRADY HOTEL *Courtesy Henry Grady Hotel*
Erected in 1924 upon the site of the old Governor's Mansion

GOVERNOR'S MANSION *Courtesy Atlanta Historical Society*
Residence of Georgia's Chief Executives from 1870 to 1921

FEDERAL BUILDING *Courtesy Atlanta Newspapers, Inc.*
Modern simplicity replaces Victorian ornateness at Peachtree and Baker

Courtesy Atlanta Historical Society
DOUGHERTY-HOPKINS HOUSE
"The House of a Thousand Candles" was built in 1890

Courtesy Atlanta Historical Society

COLONEL ROBERT J. LOWERY AND HIS FAMOUS TALLYHO

TOMPKINS-LITTLE HOUSE *Courtesy Atlanta Historical Society*

Columned splendor at the corner of Peachtree and Eighth streets

FIVE POINTS, 1892 *Courtesy Atlanta Historical Society*

ELECTRIC BUILDING *Courtesy Georgia Power Company*
At the downtown junction of the Peachtrees: Merchandise Mart

Coca-Cola ever mixed with soda water. When a customer asked that the locally popular headache remedy be mixed with water in an effort to hasten relief, Willis E. Venable, proprietor of the fountain, reached for the nearest bottle of water, which happened to be soda. He mixed it with the patent medicine and the customer drank it, declaring delightedly that it tasted fine. Soon the few other local druggists who stocked Coca-Cola were administering it in soda water.

The development of the world-famed soft drink was closely associated with Peachtree Street. Its originator, Dr. John Styth Pemberton, came to Atlanta from Columbus in 1869 and became senior member of a firm of wholesale druggists and manufacturing chemists with offices at 23-25 Peachtree, southeast corner of Line Street (now Edgewood Avenue). In 1886, after Dr. Pemberton had formed the Pemberton Chemical Company and moved from Peachtree, he developed the Coca-Cola formula, which was based upon a non-syrup medicine he had concocted at the Peachtree site. Two years later Pemberton divested himself of all rights to the product for the sum of $1,750.

The new owner was Asa Griggs Candler, a former Carroll County farm boy, who had come to Atlanta in 1873 and obtained a job at George J. Howard's drug store on the east side of Peachtree between Line and Wheat streets (the block between the present Edgewood and Auburn avenues). While working there he won the hand of his employer's daughter, Miss Lucy Elizabeth Howard. After buying a portion of Dr. Pemberton's interest and obtaining the remainder from intermediate owners, Candler owned all rights to Coca-Cola for a total investment of $2,300. Through his energy and ability the headache potion soon brought him wealth beyond his most optimistic expectations.

Despite Coca-Cola's later phenomenal success, it was of slight interest to the average Atlantian in the 'eighties, whose attention was captured and held by the heated controversy bubbling around a different type of beverage—alcohol. Under a state law permitting local option Atlanta held its first prohibition referendum in 1885. Mass meetings were conducted by those in favor of prohibition and by those opposed to it, with the "Drys" citing the evils and dangers of alcohol, and the "Wets" extolling its delights and the financial benefits which accrued to the city through its legal consumption. A count of the votes revealed that the Drys had won and after a seven-month period of grace the city's saloons closed their doors. At 52 Peachtree, M. E. Maher's saloon, like all the others, was tightly closed. Above the door to the emporium was a placard draped with crepe, which read: "Closed on account of the death of prohibition and the birth of this ruin."

Atlanta's fondness for parades was gratified by a gala celebration in honor of Grover Cleveland's election as President in 1884. To signify their elation at the election of a Democrat to the nation's highest office after a lapse of twenty-four years, the people of Atlanta indulged in a frenzy of rejoicing on Friday, November 7th. A great crowd, led by Henry W. Grady with a silk flag wrapped around his hat, swept into the Capitol and imperiously forced the adjournment of the House and the Senate.

That night the celebration got under way in earnest. Thousands of cheering Atlantians gathered in the vicinity of the *Constitution* building, their excited faces eerily illuminated by the glow of many bonfires. The music of bands, the rhythmic beat of drums, and the blare of horns added to the confusion of the scene. An impromptu parade was organized and the marchers moved into position behind sixteen mounted policemen. As the procession turned from Decatur Street into Peachtree thousands of torches in the hands of celebrants illumined the Five Points scene. Flags waved in the breeze of early evening, new bonfires were kindled, and colored lanterns were brought out. Hastily created window displays of Peachtree merchants added to the patriotic motif.

As the parade approached the residential section of Peachtree, the scene became even more spectacular. Along the gently sloping incline from Five Points to Ellis Street the flickering torches in the hands of the thousands of marchers resembled a river of fire. Every house on Peachtree was brightly lighted from within as well as from without. The lawn of the Leyden house was filled with a thousand Chinese lanterns and the sparkling glow from the nearby Capital City Club resembled the glitter from a kingly crown. The procession grew to a mile and a half in length and 25,000 people were said to have been in the streets at one time. Moving past Baker Street the procession continued along Peachtree until it reached Forrest Avenue, at which point it turned and proceeded back to town. The celebration continued until midnight, but finally the booming of cannon ceased, the bands were quiet, and the hoarse and weary Democrats of the Gate City went home to bed.

This festive parade was in contrast to a procession which had moved along Peachtree a year and a half earlier. On that occasion the body of Alexander Hamilton Stephens, Governor of Georgia and former Vice-President of the Confederacy, had been transported from the Executive Mansion to the Capitol for the homage of a sorrowful people. "Little Alec," frail and ill at seventy, had been in office only four months.

The cortège moved from the Mansion at the southwest corner of Peachtree and Cain streets. Windows, balconies, and roofs were filled with spectators. Along intersecting streets were the carriages, buggies, and wagons of many of the thousands of persons who had poured into town for the funeral. The somber procession moved slowly through the quiet throng assembled under the crepe streamers of official mourning, and all that was mortal of Alexander H. Stephens had soon passed from the scenes of his triumphs and tragedies.

Later that year gentlemen strolling along Peachtree respectfully removed their hats as another funeral procession stirred up the red dust of the thoroughfare. This was the cortège accompanying the body of Mrs. C. R. Haskins to its resting place. She was the first person to be buried in West View Cemetery, in southwest Atlanta. This gently rolling tract with its carefully tended gardens is said to be one of the most beautiful cemeteries in America. Its developers included such prominent Peachtree residents as Walker P. Inman, James R. Wylie, H. I. Kimball, Rufus B. Bullock, Willis E. Ragan, Henry H. Cabaniss, and E. P. McBurney.

In this era Atlanta acquired a second electric streetcar line which traversed Peachtree only from Broad to Houston streets. Its influence upon the lives of residents of the north-south artery, however, was felt immediately. The nine-mile route of the line originated at Marietta and Broad streets, wound along Peachtree and Houston streets to Highland and Virginia avenues and thence back to the point of origin, via Boulevard.

As *Atlanta and Environs* says of it: "The Nine-Mile Circle, fare five cents for the round trip, immediately became popular for picnic and sight-seeing parties, running as it did through the wooded northeastern section of the city and suburbs. Indeed, it became the custom during the 90's for picnic groups to charter a car, spread lunch in the woods and return to the city at dusk. On Sunday afternoons the cars on the Circle were so crowded that the seats had to be turned back to back so that the ladies could sit down and the girls stand in the space between, while the men and boys hung outside on the steps that ran the length of the car."[27]

In 1887 a group of public-spirited citizens organized the Piedmont Exposition as a showcase for the resources of the Piedmont region. The site of the mammoth undertaking was the old B. F. Walker farm, which encompassed almost 200 acres extending from Peachtree Road at the present Fourteenth Street to the Richmond & Danville Railroad tracks on the east. The organizers of the Exposition were largely the same persons who simultaneously formed the Gentlemen's Driving Club. The latter organization was created so that its members would have a suitable place in which to ride horseback and to sponsor races. The Driving Club acquired ownership of the Walker farm and agreed to lease most of it to the Piedmont Exposition Company, reserving for its own use the fieldstone Walker residence and a small surrounding acreage. Joseph Kingsberry, a native of Carrollton who was associated with the Moore-Marsh dry goods store and who was for some years a Peachtree resident, was chosen first president of the Gentlemen's Driving Club. Robert H. Richards was chosen treasurer.

The Exposition opened to a large crowd on the morning

of October 10th, and Peachtree Street was gaily decorated for the occasion. The appearance of the well-dressed throngs of country folk who strolled its sidewalks compared favorably with that of their more sophisticated city cousins.

The high point of the Piedmont Exposition came a week later when President Grover Cleveland and his bride arrived for a two-day visit. The invitation to them, issued at the suggestion of Henry W. Grady, had been engraved on sheets of gold from Dahlonega, Georgia, and enclosed in a case of hardwoods studded with precious stones. The Presidential party arrived by special train and was met by a salute of cannon, fireworks, and artillery.

Next morning the President and his lady entered a closed carriage in company with Charles A. Collier and Mr. Grady and were driven to the Exposition grounds. Despite a steady rain, the distinguished guests were welcomed by a great crowd which greeted them as they left the Kimball House and proceeded out Peachtree to Wilson Avenue (now Fourteenth Street) and thence east to the site of the Exposition. The Presidential carriage was preceded on this drive by the dashing members of the Governor's Horse Guards, handsomely mounted and gorgeously attired.

Atlanta outdid itself in entertaining the visiting chief of state and his charming young wife. The initial festivity was an elaborate dinner and reception at the Executive Mansion for the President and the men in his party. Host for this occasion was Governor John B. Gordon. The guest list was limited to visiting governors, congressmen, justices, high ranking military persons, and a select few Georgia state officials. Peachtree's two most prominent residents in attendance were Chief Justice Logan Bleckley and Henry W. Grady.

While the gentlemen were being entertained, Mrs. Cleveland and Mrs. William F. Vilas, wife of the visiting postmaster general, were accorded the hospitality of one of Peachtree's handsomest mansions. The occasion was a luncheon given by Mrs. James H. Porter, wife of the president of the Merchants Bank, at her home on the southwest corner of Peachtree and

Porter Place. In recalling the affair some years later, the hostess' daughter, Mrs. E. Bates Block, wrote:

"It was 4 o'clock when Mrs. Cleveland's escort dropped her at the door of the beautiful Porter home. . . . From the chandeliers hung smilax, and the pictures were similarly draped. Numerous cut glass bowls, filled with the rarest of cut flowers, were arranged about the room, and on the handsome lace curtains were pinned innumerable rosebuds that made them lovely beyond description. The . . . ladies invited to meet Mrs. Cleveland were gathered in the parlor opposite the one in which Mrs. Cleveland stood. This room was filled with handsome tropical plants; orange trees, on which the golden fruit was hanging; pineapple, banana plants and ferns were banked in front of the mantel, giving to the room as beautiful an appearance as rich plants artistically arranged can do. . . .

"At each plate were beautiful hand-painted favors in the form of a book, the outer coverings containing lovely pictures descriptive of southern scenery. . . .

"The table was laid with artistic effect. The cloth was composed of alternate silk stripes of red, white and blue, representing the national colors. From each chandelier were suspended large C's composed of roses; the centerpiece was a large punch bowl of cut glass, three feet across, filled with Maréchel Neil roses, and about the base was gathered blue silk upon which silver stars glistened and shone in the fairy light of the mellow lamps upon the table. In addition to the gas above, and the dozen or more fairy lamps upon the table, there were also two bronze candelabra of exquisite workmanship and proportion, each with eight branches, adding the rich light of the wax candles to the scene. In front of Mrs. Porter was an immense floral slipper, formed of exquisite rosebuds, signifying the good luck that is so often wooed by symbols and signs. At the other end, opposite Mrs. Lowry, was a beautiful floral ship with its flowing sails expanded, flying at the mast top the flag of the Union. The room was lovely with smilax; the chandeliers, mantel and pictures being hung with it.

"The table was a poem in cut glass . . . and the thousand diamond points flashed back the light of the lamps in a million hues. . . . The fruit and the usual accompaniments were upon the table, the lunch being served from the side. The first course was raw oysters and they were served from exquisite Royal Worcester China plates. The dinner and other plates were lovely, being selections of Crown Derby, Dresden, Royal Worcester, Merton and other handsome brands of china. There were twelve courses in all. At each plate were five wine glasses—for champagne, claret, punch, madeira and sherry. . . . Each wine glass was tied with a different-colored narrow silk bow. . . .

"Beyond all question, it was the handsomest lunch ever served in Atlanta. . . . It was nearly 7 o'clock when the ladies rose. . . .

"Mrs. Cleveland wore a black velvet dress trimmed with jet. Her hat, which was relieved by white ribbon, was not removed on her entrance, but was worn during the lunch. The dress was a rich-looking dress, but was of the style and kind worn by ladies having morning visits. . . ."

Invited to meet Mrs. Cleveland and Mrs. Vilas on this happy occasion were:

Mrs. John B. Gordon	Mrs. Julius Brown
Mrs. Pat Calhoun	Mrs. Henry Grady
Mrs. William Dickson	Mrs. F. C. Freeman
Mrs. T. D. Meador	Miss Annie Reid
Mrs. Henry Collier	Mrs. Walter Taylor
Mrs. Livingston Mims	Miss Sallie Johnson
Mrs. Robert Clark	Mrs. Albert Thornton
Mrs. Lewis Beck	Mrs. W. B. Lowe
Mrs. R. J. Lowry	Mrs. Joseph Thompson

Miss Mary Lou Bacon of Macon
Mrs. Mark Johnson of Macon
Mrs. Charles Phinizy of Augusta[28]

After three hours of such overpowering elegance, one would expect Mrs. Cleveland to have retired to her boudoir in the bridal suite of the Kimball House. Not so, for Peachtree had yet another affair to honor the hardy Presidential couple.

That evening some 900 members of Georgia society assembled at the Capital City Club, at the northwest corner of

Peachtree and Ellis streets. There they dined upon cold ham, turkey and tongue, turkey and chicken salads, hot and cold breads, oysters, beautifully iced cakes, and a wide variety of fruits. Champagne was available in great quantities, and claret punch, champagne punch, sherry, Madeira, and other wines were served. Following the departure of the Presidential party shortly after midnight, the artillery band changed from classical to dance music, and many of the younger guests danced until a late hour.

History does not record whether the Clevelands slept well that night, but at any rate they were up early the next day for another strenuous round of activities. The only social event which took place on Peachtree was a reception for 400 persons, at which Mrs. Henry W. Grady was hostess at her residence.

Although rain continued to fall as on the previous day, a brilliant parade was held in the downtown section that evening. Led by two snappy bands, the procession proceeded to the artesian well amid the glare of Roman candles and ten thousand flickering torches. At Five Points a mighty cheer arose before the marchers quieted and the scheduled program got under way. Because of the inclement weather Mrs. Cleveland watched the celebration from the comfort of her nearby hotel room. The President graciously acknowledged brief speeches by Governor Gordon, Mr. Grady, and others, and then returned to the Kimball House to prepare for his departure later in the evening.

Atlanta and its most famous thoroughfare have entertained a long roster of dignitaries in the years of their partnership, but none has ever quite matched the splendor attendant upon the visit of President and Mrs. Cleveland to the Piedmont Exposition of 1887.

A short while after the triumphal success of the exposition which he had fathered, Henry Grady made a sudden exit from the scenes of his labor. On December 12, 1889, he received an enthusiastic ovation at Boston following delivery of a speech upon the subject, "The Race Problem in the South." Returning to Atlanta by private railroad car five days later, he was so ill from a cold that he was unable to acknowledge the demonstration of the crowd which met him at the old car shed. He was assisted into a carriage and driven quickly to his home, 353 Peachtree Street, where his condition worsened rapidly; soon pleuro-pneumonia had set in. All through the long and anxious hours of his illness Peachtree and nearby Merritts and Linden avenues were thronged with silent watchers. Finally, early on the morning of December 23rd, the voice of the "New South's" prophet was stilled.

Henry Woodfin Grady was buried on a marvelously sunny Christmas Day. An undertaker's somber horse-drawn hearse transported the body from the residence to the First Methodist Church, where a simple service was conducted by the pastor, Dr. H. C. Morrison, assisted by other clergymen. Mr. Grady's favorite hymn, "Shall We Gather at the River," was one of four selections sung by the choir.

As the cortège moved from the church to Oakland Cemetery, where the body of the great editor reposed until a vault could be built in Westview, a silent throng of thousands lined Peachtree and adjacent streets. In the first of the many carriages in the procession were Governor John B. Gordon, Chief Justice Logan E. Bleckley, Mayor John T. Glenn, and ex-Governor Henry D. McDaniel—all of whom were Peachtree residents and long-time friends of the deceased. The silent streets had been divested of their Christmas decorations and were draped in the black and white of deep mourning. Church bells tolled continuously; the city's policemen stood in smart formation with their helmets held at their breasts; men and women—rich and poor, black and white—lined the streets and crowded into available doorways and windows. As the sound of hoofbeats faded into the distance and the winter sun set in a blaze of glory, Peachtree Street bade farewell to its most famous resident.

Due in great measure to Grady's enlightened leadership, Georgia had made painful but steady progress in rising from the ashes of the Civil War. Atlanta's resurgence and growth were notable. The evidence of war was gone in a few short years, and as the business pulse of the community quickened the city began to expand in every direction. The extension of the city limits northward to Sixth Street was directly attributable to the opening of Peters Park, which occupied the entire west side of the block between Fourth and Fifth streets. This 200-acre tract, extending from North Avenue to Eighth Street and from the rear of Richard Peters' residence to the present Atlantic Drive, had been bought by him in 1849 for a mere $900. Under the direction of Mr. Peters, real estate man George W. Adair, and the indefatigable H. I. Kimball, Peters Park was patterned after the Chicago suburb of Pullman.

Peachtree Street in those days was entering upon the period of its greatest glory as a fashionable residential thoroughfare. Great brick and stone mansions were erected in block after block of what had recently been a peaceful rural road lined with small farmhouses. "Society," which originally had sniffed at the *nouveau riche* and their gingerbread mansions, was beginning to move in increasing numbers from the decaying columned mansions south of the new Capitol and from the newer and smarter houses in West End.

Most of the new Peachtree residences were erected in the blocks between North Avenue and what had formerly been known as "Tight Squeeze" (now the Tenth Street area). Next to the E. R. DuBose home at the southeast corner of Peachtree and North Avenue was the attractive new residence of Mrs. Ellen G. McCabe, a widow who had recently arrived from Columbus, Mississippi. She moved to Atlanta to be with her son, John K. Ottley, and his first wife, who was her step-daughter. Mr. Ottley rapidly rose to a position of eminence in banking and civic affairs, and his wife became a widely known clubwoman. The Ottleys and Mrs. McCabe enjoyed great popularity in Atlanta's social circles.

A block north, at the southwest corner of Peachtree and Kimball (now Ponce de Leon Avenue), a massive three-story granite mansion was erected for Samuel Martin Inman and his young second wife, the former Mildred McPheeters of Raleigh, North Carolina. This elegantly-appointed home was a center for many of Atlanta's outstanding social functions.

Mr. Inman, a native of Dandridge, Tennessee, had come

to Atlanta in 1867 after attending Princeton and serving as a lieutenant of cavalry in the Civil War. He organized S. M. Inman & Co., which at one time was the largest cotton brokerage house in the world. In all the years of his residence in Atlanta Mr. Inman was an active, public-spirited citizen, and in the years following his retirement from business in 1896 he devoted his time and much of his fortune to the betterment of his adopted city. He was a son of Shadrach W. Inman, a nephew of Walker P. Inman, and a brother of Hugh T. Inman, Mrs. E. R. DuBose, and Miss Jennie Inman—all of whom lived on Peachtree.

One of the handsomest residences of this period was that of Captain William Greene Raoul, on the west side of Peachtree just north of Sixth Street. Designed by New York architect Bradford L. Gilbert, the three-story house of rose brick afforded every accommodation that could be desired by a large and wealthy family. In addition to entertaining rooms and guest bedrooms, there were a laundry room, a carpenter shop, and a wine cellar. At the rear of the property were a cottage for servants and a stable. Adjoining the stable was a "lot" where the family cow grazed. The most surprising feature of the establishment, according to Atlantians of the era, was a tennis court, the first such play area in Atlanta. The Raoul children were at first gently chided for participating in such a strenuous activity as tennis on Sunday mornings, but before long the game had won general acceptance among the young people of Peachtree.

Captain Raoul, president of the Mexican National Railroad, with offices in New York, had moved his family to Atlanta so that they could have the pleasures and security of a permanent home. A native of Louisiana, he had previously lived in Georgia as president of the Central Railroad and Banking Company and of various associated lines. His wife was the former Mary Millen Wadley, daughter of former Central president William M. Wadley. Captain and Mrs. Raoul had eleven children, who filled their Peachtree mansion with youthful laughter and pranks.

The Raouls' next-door neighbors to the north were Mr.

and Mrs. William Henry Inman, who lived in an attractive two-story brick house. Mr. Inman, a son of Walker P. Inman, was engaged in the cotton business. Following his death in 1902, his widow, the former Nanaline Holt of Macon, became the second wife of millionaire tobacco tycoon James Buchanan Duke. She was the mother of Doris Duke, often called "the richest girl in the world," and of Walker Patterson Inman, 2nd.

At the southwest corner of Peachtree and Eighth streets was a beautiful two-story brick mansion which had about it an aura of romance and tragedy. It was erected in 1890-91 by Colonel Leonidas A. Jordan, who did not count expense in its construction or in its furnishings. The chandeliers in the drawing room were of gold and those in the living room were of silver. One mantel alone cost $1,800, which was a small fortune in those days, and the furnishings were of the finest mahogany obtainable.

The house was built to gratify Colonel Jordan's beautiful and enormously popular wife, who wanted an Atlanta home so that she could enjoy the society of her many friends in the capital city. The couple already had a house in Columbus, a mansion in Macon, and a huge plantation near Albany. Colonel Jordan could easily afford such opulence, for when his father had died in Baldwin County prior to the Civil War he had left his only child seven plantations and more than eleven hundred slaves.

Mrs. Jordan was a remarkably beautiful woman and her beauty, added to her charm and great wealth, had made her a social favorite in the South, in the East, and in Europe. The former Julia Hurt of Columbus, she was the widow of dashing Confederate Colonel Peyton H. Colquitt. It was widely known that while living in Paris during her widowhood she had fallen in love with Jerome Napoleon Bonaparte, grand-nephew of the Emperor. Mindful of the unhappy fate of her suitor's American grandmother, however, she did not accept his proposal of marriage but returned to the United States and in 1868 was married to Colonel Jordan.

Late in December, 1891, the Jordans' handsome new house was almost ready to receive its lovely mistress. As the last pieces of furniture arrived from Cincinnati, however, tragedy struck; the beauteous Mrs. Jordan died suddenly at her home in Columbus. Her grief-stricken husband retained the new house for only a year, then sold it for $65,000, and never again lived in Atlanta. The new owners of the house were Mr. and Mrs. William M. Dickson, who previously had lived at the southwest corner of Peachtree and Cox (later Linden Avenue).

Across Eighth Street from the Jordan home was the magnificent white-columned mansion which had been erected for Judge Henry B. Tompkins and his second wife, a niece of Georgia's General Robert Toombs. It had been built on the site of a small cottage which had been occupied for ten years by Mr. and Mrs. J. W. Culpepper and their two daughters. The stately new structure, designed by Atlanta architect Walter T. Downing, had four downstairs rooms which were notable for their exceptional beauty. The reception room was decorated in yellow and furnished with fragile gilded period pieces; the sitting room was furnished in rose; the dining room had dark red walls with a stenciled design; and the oak-panelled library was decorated in green. Behind the house was a large stable with horses and carriages and above were rooms for the Tompkins' five servants. An unusual feature of the servants' quarters was a huge enameled bathtub (in a day when plumbing was a luxury) which Judge Tompkins had installed in an effort to make his servants happy. The colored retainers, apparently feeling that it would be extravagant for them to waste such a commodious item by bathing in it, used it as a storage bin for coal.

Judge Tompkins, a native of Alabama and long a distinguished Atlanta attorney, and his wife both died after living in the house less than fifteen years and it then became the residence of Mr. and Mrs. John D. Little.

Mr. Little was a native of Columbus who had served in the state legislature, after which he entered the practice of law in Atlanta. His wife, interestingly enough, was the former Ilah Dunlap of Macon, who at the age of twenty-one had become the second wife of sixty-seven-year-old Colonel Leonidas A. Jordan. The old gentleman died five years later, at which time, in accordance with a pre-marital agreement, his young wife became sole heir to his immense fortune. Thus, in becoming mistress of the Tompkins home, Mrs. Little could look upon the nearby house which her first husband had built for his adored first wife.

CHAPTER
SIX

Peachtree Kaleidoscope

WITH the addition of many handsome new residences along its tree-shaded northern extremity, Peachtree acquired a beauty and sophistication which must have flabbergasted pioneer citizen George Washington Collier as he drove his buggy in from his vast acreage near Peachtree Creek. Not only had the once tranquil farm road disappeared south of the new Bleckley Avenue (later Tenth Street, east of Peachtree), but the downtown section of Peachtree near the business district was also undergoing changes.

Atlanta acquired its most unusual structure in 1889 when a three-story triangular building was erected at the northwest corner of the Peachtree-Forsyth-Church Street (later Carnegie Way) intersection. Its façade was covered with marble slabs carved with Biblical texts, most of them advocating economy. One of the two stone blocks flanking the entrance was inscribed: "This is the House That Jack Built," while this message appeared upon the other: "J. N. Smith's Building: Commenced 100 years after George Washington's inauguration as First President—Paul says: Owe No Man:—Let Posterity Heed His Advice." Because the owner of the property craftily stipulated that these blocks must forever be a part of any building erected upon the site, they are a part of the cornice of the present structure in the heart of downtown Atlanta.

Jasper Smith, the eccentric builder of "The House That Jack Built," was himself for years one of the sights of the city.

Born in Walton County, he moved to Atlanta after the Civil War and shrewdly realized that the devastated community would need bricks to rebuild its houses and stores. For $100 an acre he bought fourteen acres in the vicinity of the present Peachtree and Fourteenth streets. There he turned out an estimated ten million bricks for the rebuilding of Atlanta before selling his brickyard for a handsome profit and investing in downtown real estate.

"Jack" Smith was a real curiosity—a man without city airs, yet an actor of no small skill who delighted in the attention which his eccentricities attracted. He was a short but imposing figure in his customary garb: a short-coated sack suit and a tall silk hat, and no necktie. A freshly starched collar was always buttoned at his throat, but he was never seen wearing a cravat. Indeed, his dislike of neckwear was carried to a ridiculous extreme. Many years before his death he designed and supervised the construction in Oakland Cemetery of his own granite mausoleum, and arranged for disposition at the proper time of the coffin which he had already selected. Atop the entrance to the mausoleum was a statue of Mr. Smith seated in an armchair and holding his familiar top hat. The statue, naturally, wore no necktie. But several years later a small vine climbed up the side of the mausoleum and attached itself to the statue's neck. When Mr. Smith heard of it he immediately journeyed to the cemetery and personally removed the offending weed.

Although Jasper Smith was the object of derisive comments during his early years in Atlanta, when it became apparent that he had become wealthy through his business acumen the hoots turned into murmurs of respect. In his later years he was often referred to as "Atlanta's quaintest character."

In the block immediately to the north of "The House That Jack Built" the ornate R. H. Richards mansion acquired a new master in 1895 when Mr. Richards' widow became the second wife of Benjamin F. Abbott. Mr. Abbott, a native of Cherokee County and a veteran of service in the Army of Northern Virginia, was one of Atlanta's most distinguished attorneys. His first wife, the former Belle Kendrick of Atlanta,

RESIDENCE OF JOHN W. GRANT *Courtesy Atlanta Historical Society*
Next to the home of his grandfather, John T. Grant, southeast corner of Pine Street

ARAGON HOTEL *Courtesy Atlanta Historical Society*
Fence at left surrounds Maddox home at northeast corner of Ellis Street

RESIDENCE OF GEORGE WINSHIP *Courtesy Atlanta Historical Society*

Courtesy Howell House

HOWELL HOUSE WHERE ONCE MRS. WINSHIP'S ROSES BLOOMED

PETERS RESIDENCE *Courtesy Atlanta Historical Society*
Built by pioneer citizen Richard Peters in 1881

FIRST BAPTIST CHURCH *Courtesy First Baptist Church*
On the former site of the Peters home

HOME OF MAJOR JOHN S. COHEN *Courtesy Atlanta Historical Society*
Built by his father-in-law, Robert C. Clarke, at Peachtree Place

RESIDENCE OF FLEMING G. duBIGNON *Courtesy Atlanta Historical Society*
Site now occupied by the Miller Building, near Fourteenth Street

had acquired a modest reputation as an author, her best-known novel being *Leah Mordecai.* The home of Colonel Abbott and his first wife, located on the east side of Peachtree in the middle of the block between Cain and Harris streets, subsequently became the home of Dr. W. S. Elkin, Jr.

The last of the great houses to be built on the oldest section of Peachtree was constructed in 1890, at the southeast corner of Peachtree and Baker streets. It was built for David H. Dougherty, a leading dry goods merchant, on the site of his earlier one-story bungalow—property which had once been a part of pioneer settler Hardy Ivy's farm. The turreted castle which Mr. Dougherty built on his red clay hill overlooking the junction of the Peachtrees was a romantic edifice with towers, porches, dormers, and balconies giving it the appearance of a Swiss chalet. The central hallway was a splendid three-story affair onto which private balconies opened from rooms on the second and third floors. The focal point of the entire house was a magnificent crystal chandelier suspended from the roof and extending through a gracefully spiraling stairway to the reception hall. When it was lighted its glittering splendor gave the effect of myriads of candles—thus giving the place its name of "The House of a Thousand Candles."

In the 'nineties Atlanta enjoyed the greatest prosperity it had ever known. Memories of the late unpleasantness with the "Nawth" began to dim somewhat as the city expanded and as the horizons of its residents began to widen. Social activity assumed an unusual importance, and frequent balls, debut parties, and wedding "collations" served as appropriate backgrounds for Peachtree's beautiful women.

A rigid set of rules governed social intercourse and even minor infractions caused the name of the violator to be scratched from the guest list which each hostess maintained. One can imagine, therefore, with what mirth "Society" heard of an aspiring young man, who upon being extended a third-person invitation by the wife of a business acquaintance, wrote in reply: "Dear Sir and Wife. I'll be there on time. Respect'fly yrs."[29]

Peachtree matrons of the period had certain days on which

they received their friends, who spent a portion of each day in calling upon those who were "At Home." This custom had been introduced to Atlanta by Mrs. William Greene Raoul when she returned from living in New York. Dressed in the latest fashions, the callers were met at the front door of each house by a butler or maid. After leaving cards for the ladies of the house, exchanging the latest gossip, and sampling the delicacies spread upon the dining room table, they decorously entered their carriages and moved on to other houses.

One of the favorite forms of amusement for Peachtree's young people in those days of innocent diversion was the afternoon drive. William G. Raoul, Jr., a popular man of the era, later wrote of this activity:

"Around four o'clock, of a summer's afternoon, all the smart traps of the street turned out with their gay and carefree drivers and their parties. A buggy was taboo. No girl was allowed to take a 'buggy ride,' but a 'trap' was quite all right. Usually we went in fours in smart heavily built traps. . . . Up and down Peachtree we paraded, bowing low as we passed; seeing and being seen. Then, all wound up at the Piedmont Driving Club. Sitting at tables on the broad open porches, we drank our juleps and chatted nonsense. . . ."[30]

One of Atlanta's greatest beaus in the 'nineties was Telamon Cruger Cuyler Smith, whose wealthy and popular parents, Mr. and Mrs. Henry H. Smith, lived at the site of the present Ponce de Leon Apartments. The Smith home had the first upholstered porch furniture in Atlanta, made of gay cotton from India which Mrs. Smith bought in London and had Atlanta upholsters use on a lounge of her own design. The son of the household differed with young Mr. Raoul about ladies not riding in buggies, for in his old age he wrote:

"Livery stables had many buggies for rent and fellows took their best girls out driving on all fair summer days to Ponce de Leon Springs [site of the present Sears, Roebuck and the old baseball park on Ponce de Leon Avenue], Buckhead, Hapeville and along the winding roads to the river. . . .

"Buggies were mostly done in green or black, with a few in yellow, but one in flaming red was the best known in Atlanta. It had the first rubber tires I ever saw on a buggy. That was the famous buggy in which 'Cap' Joyner, chief of the Atlanta Fire Department, dashed ahead of his galloping fire engines, hook-and-ladder trucks and hose wagons whenever the bell at headquarters rang out an alarm. I have seen 'Cap' go madly along, bumping high as he hit a car track, swaying perilously on sharp turns as he and his aide literally flew apart. We all cheered 'Cap' for he deserved all our praise and affection. . . .

"The carts which other young men and I used to drive about Atlanta in 1895 were so high that we installed blocks at the curb in front of our homes to use as steps.

"We were proud of our turn-outs back in those days. They were kept varnished and polished, always freshly washed. The harness required infinite care. . . .

"We took lessons in riding and driving. We learned how to handle reins and whip with skill and grace, how to turn in a narrow street.

"We were proud when we mastered the 15-foot whip used in driving tandem—a wheel horse with a leader in front.

"Driving tandem required infinite skill, for a faulty turn would upset the cart and spill its passengers.

"The driver and his fair guest sat in front, with a small negro groom on the rear seat, facing backward. He wore immaculate white buckskin breeches, top boots, a green coat and a low-crowned silk hat. It was his duty when the cart stopped to jump down smartly and take the bridle of the leader. . . .

"Pony carts, governess' carts, basket carts and Shetland ponies once dotted Atlanta's tree-shaded streets. . . . A handsome, $2,400 brougham from the shop of John Smith, the 'class' carriage builder, was double-doored, with a front of glass and upholstered in blue leather and silk. It held only two, and when 'balloon sleeves' widened a foot out from a lady's shoulder, the man had to sit forward to give her room.

"Just think of a carriage, $1,200; horses, $700; harness, $400;

coachman's outfit, $100. Very few people had 'em! Good stables out Peachtree represented outlays of $12,000 to $20,000! . . .

"When Mrs. W. D. Grant, Mrs. W. B. Lowe or Mrs. Henry B. Tompkins gave a tea, broughams, landaus and open victorias lined up on both sides of Peachtree for several blocks.

"Willis Ragan's mansion was where the Fox movie is now and he had two broughams, a landau, a victoria and four carts. . . ."[31]

Perhaps the grandest spectacle in all of Atlanta was Colonel Robert J. Lowry, wealthy banker and distinguished civic and social leader, speeding out Peachtree in his splendid "tallyho." The huge coach of maroon and silver was usually pulled by four fine white bay horses and the harness was fit for a king. Sometimes a magnificently garbed coachman sat in the driver's seat and handled the reins, but often Colonel Lowry would take over this chore. Two small Negro footmen rode on the high seat at the rear of the coach.

The first coach which Colonel Lowry owned was acquired shortly before the International Cotton Exposition of 1881. When thousands of visitors trooped into Atlanta for the "fair," one of the sights they gawked at was the handsome coach. One whiskery old mountaineer from East Tennessee turned to an acquaintance and said, "Ain't Bob Lowry got enough money 'thout drivin' er stage?"[32]

It was said that Colonel Lowry had acquired his love for horses and coaches when as a boy in his native Greenville, Tennessee, he watched the stage coaches wheel into town, their arrival heralded by the sound of a bugle. Young Bob Lowry determined that when he was a man he would have a coach and four. And, indeed, he did. His elegant equipage was so much finer than any he had seen in his boyhood, however, that no comparison was possible. But always (and this but added to the glamor) his passage along Peachtree was announced by the clear tones of a silver bugle blown by his own personal bugler.

Colonel Lowry drove with a consummate skill. When his coach was filled with pretty debutantes on summer afternoons, people would stop and pull off the city streets and country roads to let him pass, while applauding his admirable handling of the reins. There on the box of his tallyho he was like a boy, filled with the enthusiasm of youth, his handsome face wreathed in a smile of delight.

As freshly starched little girls sat primly on front steps late in the afternoons to watch the people of Peachtree go by, a cry would go up at dusk, "The tallyho, the tallyho!" The young ladies, no longer so sedate, would jump up and down and squeal in delight. As the beautiful horses, the magnificent vehicle, and the distinguished Colonel sailed past, the girls caught glimpses of a succession of lovely creatures inside who seemed to have stepped from a Gainsborough portrait.

Winter and summer, rain or shine, "Colonel Bob" and his tallyho provided Atlanta with an exciting and splendid sight. For twenty years he played host to debutantes, distinguished visitors, and actors and actresses who graced the local theater. Always they rode in the tallyho, and nearly always they wound up at the Driving Club as guests of Robert Lowry. The diary in which the genial sportsman recorded the names of his guests reads like a listing of the famous personages of the 'eighties and 'nineties.

Atlanta society turned out *en masse* on February 10, 1893, for the formal opening of Laurent DeGive's Grand Theater, located at the southeast corner of Peachtree, Banks Place, and Pryor Street. It was a gala occasion which brought forth beautiful gowns, magnificent jewels, countless bouquets, and the elegant black and white of masculine evening attire. A sensation was created by the new electric lights which illumined the opera house, and it was confidently predicted that soon Atlanta's gas-lit residences would have the new convenience. The fresh scenery and the handsome interior provided an appropriate setting for the new Belasco-DeMille play *Men and Women*, just come from a successful run in New York.

Among well-known Peachtree residents occupying boxes for the occasion were: Mr. and Mrs. Henry H. Cabaniss, Mr. and Mrs. James R. Gray, Mr. and Mrs. William A. Hemphill, Mr. and Mrs. Clark Howell, Mr. and Mrs. William H. Inman, Mr. and Mrs. Thomas Cobb Jackson, Mr. and Mrs. Thomas D. Meador, Mr. and Mrs. James H. Porter, and others.

A short block north of the Grand, George Washington Collier had recently constructed a $250,000 hotel—the Aragon. This was the third hostelry to be erected on Peachtree, the first having been the National Hotel, at 2 Peachtree, and the second the Normandie, opened in 1891, at the point formed by the intersection of Peachtree and West Peachtree. A year or two after Collier's hotel was built the National was converted to offices and the Normandie was renamed the Neinmeister II.

As business had gradually crept along both sides of Peachtree as far as Ellis Street, Wash Collier had received several offers for his property on the southeast corner at the intersection of the two streets. Mr. Collier, however, was a buyer of land and never a seller. The story is told that an Eastern capitalist offered to let him name his price for the site, but he refused to do so. Finally, in a last desperate attempt to obtain the tract, the Easterner asked whether the property could be his if he covered it with silver dollars. Mr. Collier considered this surprising offer for a few minutes, then informed the would-be purchaser that he would sell provided the silver dollars were stood on edge. The Easterner gave up in defeat.

The Aragon was a six-story red brick structure with 125 rooms, and it immediately became the place to stay in Atlanta. It also had another distinction: the furniture was ordered all the way from Michigan! The hotel was famous for its cuisine. Specialties of the well-ordered dining room were lobster Newburg, hot oyster loaves, and succulent sirloin steaks. A carefully stocked wine cellar afforded a rare variety of vintage champagnes, wines, and liqueurs.

The Aragon was for many years the scene of fashionable social affairs, including wedding receptions, dinner parties, and balls. Only a month after the grand opening, Henry H. Cabaniss, an owner of the *Atlanta Journal*, was host at the first private dance held there, honoring Vice-President-Elect Adlai E. Stevenson. A few years later Mr. Cabaniss' daughter, Mildred, made her debut there amid masses of bouquets from admiring swains. She later reigned for many years as queen of the *Journal's* society department and was noted for her concise recollections of almost every Atlantian's ancestry. Her sharp and witty tongue shattered the aspirations of many a social climber who sought to improve upon the family tree.

Atlanta in those days was still very much a place where who one's forebears had been was the criterion for determining social acceptability. In the impoverished years immediately following the Civil War Southerners generally could take no pride in new houses, elaborate entertainments, superior educations for their sons and daughters, or worldly wealth, and they therefore relied upon their families' established positions as a means of maintaining their traditional status in society. The ritual of dusting the ancestral altars involved an astounding number of aunts, uncles, first cousins, cousins-twice-removed, cousins-in-law, and "kissin' cousins." The latter category included those persons who were actually remote relatives or merely old friends.

The year 1894 marked the debut of a new type of newspaper, a scandal sheet devoted to gossip and sensation. Named *The Looking-Glass*, it was widely condemned—and never more fervently than by those whose indiscretions had been reported in its columns. Reputations were shattered by its revelations, which only added to the delight with which prim matrons surreptitiously perused it in the privacy of their boudoirs.

Despite its increasing sophistication, Atlanta continued to derive an almost child-like pleasure from watching parades and participating in large public gatherings. The 'nineties provided ample opportunities for enjoying both.

A handsome bronze figure of Henry W. Grady was dedicated at the Forsyth-Marietta Street intersection late in 1891. Financed entirely by contributions from all over the country, the $20,000 monument was unveiled by the late editor's only daughter, Miss Gussie Grady, before a throng of 25,000 persons. The ceremony was preceded by a long parade which started near the new Capitol, moved out Pryor Street to Peachtree, and down Peachtree to Marietta Street.

In this era, too, Atlanta's civic spirit reached full-blown maturity. The Chamber of Commerce and its leading supporters provided the impetus for growth and, perhaps equally important, for telling the world about the advantages afforded by the Gate City of the South. Widely publicized efforts in the latter category prompted an Augusta editor to write that, "If Atlanta could suck like she can blow, the Savannah River would be running down Peachtree Street."[33]

In 1895 a magnificent show known by the formidable title of Cotton States and International Exposition was presented at the Piedmont Exposition grounds (later Piedmont Park). It was designed to display the resources of the cotton states and to stimulate trade with South American countries. In the three months of its operation, 800,000 visitors viewed its 6,000 exhibits and thousands of newspaper stories were written about it in many parts of the world. For an expenditure of less than $3,000,000, Atlanta announced to the world that an industrial giant was awakening.

Two mammoth parades along Peachtree and Wilson Avenue (Fourteenth Street) attracted great throngs to the Exposition. The first parade was in honor of the Liberty Bell, which was transported from Philadelphia by a group of citizens and a small unit of policemen. The second was in honor of Grover Cleveland, who had returned to the White House for his second term as President. Mr. Cleveland, who had officially opened the Exposition by use of a telegraph key in his home, arrived in Atlanta on October 22nd and was taken immediately to his suite at the Aragon. That evening he was guest of honor at a dinner which Mayor Porter King gave at the hotel.

On the following evening, after a gala day at the fair, the President was guest of honor at an elaborate reception at the Capital City Club. This brilliant affair attracted some one thousand guests, and the President was all smiles as he renewed acquaintances with men and women whom he had met during his earlier visit to Atlanta.

Atlanta was indebted to two noted Peachtree residents for their roles in the Cotton States Exposition. The first of these was William A. Hemphill, business manager of the *Constitution* and formerly mayor of Atlanta. He it was who conceived the idea for the Exposition and who served as temporary president of the sponsoring organization. Long a valued citizen of Atlanta, he lived on the west side of Peachtree in the block between Cox (Linden) Avenue and North Avenue. He was noted for his handsome whiskered face, his geniality, his business acumen, his civicmindedness, and for having buried three wives and married a fourth.

The second Peachtree resident who played an important role in the Exposition was Samuel M. Inman, who supported Mr. Hemphill in backing the undertaking and who served as chairman of the financial committee of the resulting organization. His most notable contribution came later when it was found that the Exposition had not been a financial success. Desiring to preserve Atlanta's financial integrity, he averted bankruptcy by offering to advance $50,000 if the other directors would advance an equal amount. This they did. Mr. Inman's public-spirited act saved the day for Atlanta and the Cotton States Exposition.

Among the hundreds of prominent figures who passed Peachtree's handsome residences en route to the fair were: Governor William McKinley of Ohio, soon to become President; Lieutenant General John M. Schofield, U.S.A.; Lieutenant General James B. Longstreet, C.S.A.; Vice-President Adlai Stevenson; Mrs. Potter Palmer, reigning Chicago social queen; Booker T. Washington, principal of Tuskeegee Institute; Walter Damrosch, orchestra conductor; and bandleaders John Philip Sousa and Victor Herbert.

Among other noted visitors of this era was Mrs. Susan B. Anthony, militant woman suffragist, who was a guest at the Aragon while in Atlanta at a convention in behalf of her movement. Many delegates to the convention, over which she presided, arrived by train and, scorning the porters at the depot, trooped along Pryor and Peachtree streets with their little black satchels clutched determinedly in their hands.

From the ante-bellum days when Mr. and Mrs. William Crisp entertained Atlantians, a steady stream of thespians, musicians, and opera singers had been attracted to the city. In the 'nineties one of the world's greatest opera singers, the "divine" Adelina Patti, maintained a suite at the Aragon. Her ties with Atlanta were close, and a devoted following regularly accorded her a royal reception when she was in residence. Her rooms were used from time to time to accommodate such renowned artists as Lillian Nordica, Edwin Booth, and others.

Miss Patti's favorite nephew, Alfredo Barili, had been a resident of Atlanta since 1880. He was a gifted Florentine, whose musical talents delighted and educated the people of his adopted city for more than fifty years. Although he was not a Peachtree resident, he was for several decades a teacher of piano and composition at Miss Ballard's fashionable Atlanta Female Institute, located in the middle of the block on the east side of Peachtree between Cain and Harris streets, and at Washington Seminary. Subsequently he formed the Barili School of Music, which he presided over until he was tragically killed by an automobile in 1935.

Another noted educational institution of the 'nineties was Miss Thornbury's select English and French School, located at the southwest corner of Peachtree and Pine streets. There, young ladies from Atlanta's leading families studied languages, history, literature, and the domestic and social arts. Upon graduation they were considered ready to take their places in the gay whirl of Society.

It was still considered unsuitable for well-bred young ladies to work, but a few daring souls ventured into the world of business with no apparent ill effects. There was a noticeable restlessness with the fettered status of womanhood, and this may have been an important factor behind the organization of several women's groups which espoused "causes" or which sought to elevate their members in one way or another.

One such organization was the Atlanta Woman's Club, which was organized in 1896 at the home of Mrs. William B. Lowe. The organization sought to bring together women from all walks of life for the purpose of social fellowship, and better understanding of and participation in the civic, legislative, and philanthropic activities of their growing city. The early meetings were held at the Lowe residence, located in the middle of the east side of the block between Linden and North avenues, and permanent quarters were later acquired on the fifth floor of the Grand Theater Building.

The Every Saturday Club was organized in 1894 as a social and history study group. It has continued to this day to maintain a small membership, although the original aura of social exclusiveness has diminished. It was organized in the residence of Mrs. Isaac S. Boyd, second wife of a prominent Atlanta furniture manufacturer and herself a former member of Nashville's literary set. The Boyds lived for several years on Peachtree in a house across from the Raoul home between Sixth and Seventh streets.

One of the most widely admired and beloved figures of this period was Major Livingston Mims, the former Mississippi attorney who made a great success as an insurance man in Atlanta. Majestic in appearance, with wide shoulders and a superb head of white hair, he had an expressive face and graceful air.

The Major's popularity was instantaneous upon his arrival in Atlanta. When the Capital City Club was organized, soon after he came, he was unanimously elected its first president—although he had not even been a member of the club. His attractive yellow frame home at the northeast corner of Peachtree and Ponce de Leon Avenue, with its gay striped awnings and colorful flower beds, was the scene of some of Atlanta's most elegant social affairs. Major Mims and his charming wife entertained often and lavishly and their reputation as gourmets *par excellence* was substantiated by their dinner parties.

Debonair, effervescent, and uninhibited though he was, Livingston Mims was also a social autocrat who firmly divided his public and business life from the life he knew as a *bon vivant* of Atlanta society. When he engaged in a pyrotechnical race for mayor at the age of seventy, he was interrupted at a mass meeting by a seedy looking character who said in a loud voice: "Major, you say you are a friend of the laboring man. Would you ask me to have dinner at your home?"

The candidate looked the man straight in the eye and said,

"Why, Hell no! You wouldn't know how to use the knives and forks on my table."

The heckler retired amid great applause for Major Mims, who shortly thereafter was elected mayor of Atlanta.

The Major was a man of great and sonorous profanity when the mood and circumstances so moved him. His neighbor Mrs. Samuel M. Inman used to relate with a twinkle in her eyes that on one occasion he came to her and said, "Well, Mrs. Inman, my wife has at last cured me of swearing."

"How did she accomplish that?" inquired Mrs. Inman.

The Major reflected for a moment, then replied imperturbably, "Damned if I remember."[34]

Then, as now, Atlanta was widely known for the charm and beauty of its women. They provided the tranquil home life, planned the elegant social affairs, and discreetly supported the successful men for which Atlanta acquired a nationwide reputation. Their contribution to the progress of their city cannot be measured easily.

It is to her men, however, that Atlanta owes the greater debt. Without their confidence, ability, venturesomeness, and cooperative effort the city might well have remained nothing more than an important rail terminus of several thousand persons. In their business life they were able and hardworking, in their public or civic life they were tireless and enthusiastic, and in their family and social life they were charming and delightful.

Peachtree Street, first because of its fashionable residential district and later because of its burgeoning business and financial district, provided Atlanta with a majority of its leaders. In regard to wealth, charm, and elegance, the residents of Peachtree between 1885 and 1910 reigned with unquestioned supremacy.

CHAPTER
SEVEN

Music in the Street

IN THE waning years of the nineteenth century Atlanta was visited by many persons of national prominence. They arrived, were toured and fêted, and they departed; all of them were quoted as being charmed by the graciousness of their hosts and by the opulence of the Peachtree mansions in which they were entertained.

In 1898 the city was the site of the eighth annual reunion of the United Confederate Veterans, of which General John B. Gordon was commander-in-chief. Some 65,000 visitors descended upon the capital city between July 20th and July 23rd for the reunion in the Exposition buildings at Piedmont Park. Among the many distinguished guests who attended the affair were Confederate Generals Gordon, Clement A. Evans, Wade Hampton, Charles G. Hooker, Stephen D. Lee, and James Longstreet, who joined their old comrades-in-arms in reminiscing about the glorious days of old and in visiting battle sites in and near Atlanta.

Atlanta was crowded with thousands of visitors in addition to the veterans and their families. Many had come seventy-five miles or more by train or wagon to catch a glimpse of the aging warriors in their gray uniforms. The crowd was so dense and accommodations so limited that many Atlantians put chairs and benches in their front yards for the comfort of the weary, dusty onlookers. Even on fashionable Peachtree many home-owners had tents erected on front lawns where transients without hotel rooms could sleep at night.

The highlight of the four-day gathering occurred on July 22nd, the thirty-fourth anniversary of the Battle of Atlanta, when the old soldiers paraded down Peachtree and other streets in a heavy rain. Proud and undaunted, they marched spiritedly to the music of "Dixie" and passed in review before bareheaded old General Gordon on his coal black horse. Now and then they wiped water from their faces and wrung out their coats, but in the presence of tens of thousands of drenched onlookers the remnants of the Confederacy passed muster with cheers of admiration ringing in their ears.

The great horde of veterans who came to Atlanta for the reunion were entertained at breakfasts, luncheons, dinners, barbecues, balls, and receptions which ranged from utter simplicity to the epitome of elegance. Among Peachtree residents who were hosts at social affairs were Dr. and Mrs. J. S. Todd, whose house was on the east side of the street between Baker Street and Porter Place; Mr. and Mrs. William Lawson Peel, whose house was at the northeast corner of Merritts Avenue; Mr. and Mrs. Eugene C. Spalding, residents of the east side of Peachtree near the eastern terminus of Howard (now Prescott) Street; Mrs. Ellen G. McCabe, who lived next to the southeast corner of North Avenue; Major and Mrs. Livingston Mims, who resided at the northeast corner of Ponce de Leon Avenue; and Mr. and Mrs. Frank Ellis, who lived on the east side of the street just north of Tenth Street. One of the largest social affairs of the four days was the reception at which General and Mrs. Clement A. Evans entertained at their home on the east side of Peachtree between Pine Street and Merritts Avenue. An estimated 5,000 persons called to pay their respects to the guest of honor, Mrs. Thomas J. Jackson—widow of the famous "Stonewall."

The *Richmond Times* called the Atlanta reunion the greatest ever and noted with some surprise that it was also the first to arouse resentment and animosity in the North. Some people above the Mason and Dixon Line contended that the South could not be loyal to the Union at the same time it was making its obeisance to the flag of the Confederacy.[35]

Five months later, following an interlude in which Atlantians had an opportunity to recover from the excitement of the Confederate reunion, the city once again was host to a large number of visiting dignitaries. The Atlanta Peace Jubilee, held at Piedmont Park on December 14th and 15th, commemorated American victory in the brief Spanish-American War. Heading the group of eminent visitors were President William McKinley, Captain Richmond Pearson Hobson, and General Joseph Wheeler. On the first afternoon of the Jubilee the Atlanta Relief Association, which had been organized by a group of socially prominent maidens to raise funds for indigent Georgia servicemen, entertained at a reception honoring the guests. The affair was held at Mr. and Mrs. William A. Hemphill's residence, an attractive two-story frame house on the west side of Peachtree between Linden Street and North Avenue. This was the only private function to which President McKinley accepted an invitation and he received an enthusiastic welcome from the hostesses and the large group of civic, military, and social leaders invited to meet him.

Atlanta's most exciting incident relating to the Spanish-American War occurred on October 26, 1899, when the State of Georgia honored a native son with a magnificent ceremony and parade. The honor guest was Lieutenant Thomas M. Brumby of Marietta, who had been Admiral Dewey's flag officer at the Battle of Manila Bay. It was he who had drawn plans for the battle, shared with Dewey the directing of the encounter which defeated the Spanish navy, and raised the United States flag over the Philippines.

At a joint session of the senate and house the General Assembly acclaimed the modest young hero for his bravery, and the governor presented him a jeweled sword from the people of Georgia. Following the ceremony at the Capitol the lieutenant took his place in a huge parade which moved to a reviewing stand at the intersection of Peachtree Street and Ponce de Leon Avenue. The route took him past the Peachtree site where he and his family had lived while his father, Colonel Anoldus V. Brumby, was fighting in the Civil War. The parade included bands, Confederate veterans, military companies, and a large contingent of local, state, and national political figures. The entire length of Peachtree from Five Points to the reviewing stand was lined with double rows of school children who excitedly waved miniature flags and pictures of Lieutenant Brumby as he passed before them. The *Atlanta Journal* said in a front page devoted exclusively to "Brumby Day," "Never before has such an array of distinguished Georgians greeted any man as assembled in Atlanta today to greet young Brumby. Senators Bacon and Clay, Congressmen Lester and Lewis and Livingston and Maddox and Adamson and Howard and Fleming and Griggs and Tate, all are here and are taking a fitting part in extending Georgia's glad hand of welcome to her worthy son. . . .

"Five thousand visitors spent last night in Atlanta, and the early morning trains brought thousands more. At noon today . . . the streets were congested with humanity. And what a good-natured, joyous crowd! . . .

"Atlanta early donned her gayest attire. In accordance with the governor's proclamation the day is being observed as a holiday, and for the time practically all business has been suspended. Bunting and flags, the same flag that Brumby planted at Manila, are flying from nearly every home and business house, and young and old alike are wearing the Brumby buttons as an illustration of their interest in the man and the occasion.

"With Brumby the day has been an eventful one. He was astir early at his rooms at the Aragon, despite the late reception at the Capital City Club rooms [on Peachtree Street] last night, and his friends began to call as early as 8 o'clock. At 10 o'clock the committee, headed by Mayor Woodward, called, and at 10:15 the party began the drive to the governor's parlors at the capitol. Along the route the young lieutenant was given one continuous ovation. Along Peachtree to Broad the carriage proceeded through a mass of cheering, shouting people, and the brave young officer was moved by the plaudits. . . ."[36]

Two brief months after the tumultuous reception Lieutenant Brumby died in Washington, at the age of forty-four. His body was returned to Georgia where it lay in state in the

Capitol prior to a funeral service at St. Philip's Episcopal Church. Burial was in Oakland Cemetery, but later the remains were removed to Westview Cemetery and interred under a granite obelisk. His jeweled sword was presented to the United States Naval Academy by his family.

As the nineteenth century ran its course Atlantians regarded with pride several new structures which added bulk and dignity to the city. Inevitably, most of them were erected on Peachtree Street—the thoroughfare of which natives proudly boasted when absent and to which they invariably took visitors when at home.

An impressive structure added to the downtown scene in this period was the English-American Building, which was erected in the triangle formed by the junction of Peachtree and Broad streets. Rising twelve stories above the upper reaches of Peachtree, it was for many years a dominant landmark. In succeeding years it bore several names, one of which—Flatiron Building—caught the popular fancy and remained in use long after the structure was renamed. The seven-story Peters Building, erected at No. 1 Peachtree by the estate of Richard Peters, was built beside the railroad tracks upon property which had long been owned by the railroad and by Peters' father-in-law, Dr. Joseph Thompson. It extended back to within three feet of the Kimball House – which soon added a Peachtree entranceway just north of the new building.

The head of Peachtree Street acquired a new bonnet in 1901 when the railroad tracks were bridged. Long the scene of frequent accidents and occasional deaths, the tracks had become a public nuisance as well as a hazard to safety. When trains pulled into the car shed, cinders and soot were showered upon passers-by as coaches and freight cars blocked traffic for many precious minutes. The opening of the $76,000 viaduct was an occasion for rejoicing by all Atlantians who had been endangered or inconvenienced by the "Iron Monsters." The new bridge served to unite the north and south sides of the city, which had long been rent by jealousy and competition.

The buildings on the west side of Peachtree between the

viaduct and Marietta Street were destroyed in an early morning fire less than a year after the opening of the viaduct. Among the structures destroyed were the old National Hotel building and the Norcross Building, both of which had been built immediately following the Civil War. The Peachtree Arcade was later erected upon the hotel site and Jonathan Norcross' ancient structure was replaced by the sixteen-story home of the Fourth National Bank. The latter was an ornate building in the Italian Renaissance style and was for years the most imposing building in Atlanta.

The Fourth National Bank's president was James W. English, its vice-president was James R. Gray, and its cashier was young John K. Ottley. The last two men were Peachtree residents whose eminence in the realms of banking, publishing, civic affairs, and society lay ahead. Captain English, the president, was a controversial figure whose detractors never forgot—or forgave—the fact that his considerable fortune had its genesis in cheap convict labor. But even his detractors admitted that English had taken an aggressive interest in the affairs of his adopted city and that as mayor in 1881, and later as police commissioner, he had actively crusaded against gambling and prostitution. His business ability commanded respect, for he had been a poor orphan in his native Louisiana at fourteen, after which he obtained employment as a buggy trimmer in Griffin, Georgia. He settled in Atlanta after the Civil War and began a steady rise in business, civic, and political affairs.

The Capital City Club had a rival for a short time early in the twentieth century when a group of socially prominent young men organized the Colonial Club. They established themselves in the "House of a Thousand Candles," the castle formerly occupied by David H. Dougherty at the southeast corner of Peachtree and Baker streets. There the members entertained at lavish balls and parties which were graced by beautiful and popular young women of Atlanta's most select circles. After only a year of gaiety, however, the Colonial blades sold the house for a mere $260 less than the $25,000 they had paid for it. The buyer was John R. Hopkins, who had acquired a fortune through the manufacture and sale of a product for removing the kink from Negroes' hair.

A social and cultural event of 1900 was the recital given at the Grand Theater on February 22nd by Ignace Jan Paderewski, Poland's brilliant young pianist—and future president—who created a sensation with his interpretation of the music of Beethoven, Schumann, Liszt, and others. A highlight of the evening's performance was the playing of Paderewski's own Minuet in A Major. Sustained applause and many enthusiastic "bravos" attested to Atlanta's pleasure in his magical music.

Later in the year the Aragon Hotel, which had recently acquired competition when the Majestic opened a scant half block to the north, was the scene of an unusual gathering. For three days (July 19th through July 21st) veterans of the Union and Confederate armies who had participated in one or more of the three major battles around Atlanta thirty-six years earlier held a reunion and toured the battle sites. A "campfire," at which Peachtree residents William A. Hemphill and Robert F. Maddox welcomed the visitors, was held at the Grand Theater on the evening of the 19th. The enthusiastic old warriors responded with deafening applause and roars of appreciation as they were read a telegram from President William McKinley and a poem written by Frank L. Stanton. Their excitement was unbounded when brief speeches were delivered by Generals John B. Gordon, Albert D. Shaw, and J. C. Breckinridge.

A house closely associated with the Civil War became a boarding house in 1893 when the Austin Leyden family, being in reduced circumstances, rented most of their beautiful house to Mrs. Emma Bell. The fine old home had been damaged severely by two fires in the 'eighties. After the first fire, which destroyed the roof, Major and Mrs. Leyden had the place rebuilt as a three-story structure with a mansard roof and a coat of green paint. A storm of protests arose from all over the city at this desecration of the beautiful and historic house, and it was regarded as no more than a just retribution when another fire burned away the second and third stories. This time the house was restored to its original height and was painted white as before.

When Mrs. Bell moved into the Leyden house, Peachtree Street acquired a new resident whose talent for homemaking and capacity for encouraging struggling young businessmen were to become legendary. Mrs. Bell had taken boarders since being widowed at the age of twenty-four some fifteen years earlier, and her establishment was first cousin to a select private club. The Bell House, as it was known throughout its long history in a series of different locations, was no ordinary boarding house. A prospective resident needed the recommendations of three "members" in good standing before his name was added to a long waiting list. When finally his name came up for nomination he was passed upon by an executive committee, after which Mrs. Bell herself decided whether the man was acceptable. If she felt an applicant was not entirely suitable, she forthrightly told him, "Young man, this is no place for you."

The standards of the Bell House were high and its rules, while few in number, were rigidly enforced. No drinking was permitted in the house, a coat was always worn downstairs and on the veranda, and smoking was not permitted in the dining rooms. Boarders were required to order their meals while seated in the living room; only when a man's meal was served at his own table was he invited into the dining room. The Bell House was justly noted for the excellence of its cuisine (a high-flown term for boarding house food, but the Bell House *was* high flown), and Mrs. Bell was quick to notice if a boarder was absent at mealtime. If he missed one meal, she wanted to know why; if he missed several, she would tell him that if he did not care to come to meals he'd best find another place to eat.

From the days of the original Bell House "boys"—Tom Paine, later a wealthy capitalist and social leader on two continents; Jack Harris; and "Cap" W. R. Joyner, Atlanta's colorful fire chief—to the last who bore the name, the gentler sex said with a sigh that once a man got settled at the Bell House there was no prying him loose. As Elinor Hillyer wrote in the old *Atlanta Journal Magazine* in 1929, "Being an ex-Bell House boy is something like Roman citizenship, a thing to be proud of, a thing with just a touch of distinction in it. A man may not have been under the old roof for a decade or more, but he will still tell you with pride and affection in his voice, 'I used to live at the Bell House.' "[37]

Another noted institution came into being on December 4, 1898, when a group of local Presbyterians met at the Peachtree residence of Walker P. Inman and organized the North Avenue Presbyterian Church. Two years later the first service was held in the handsome sanctuary which had been erected on the former site of the Edwin R. DuBose home, southeast corner of Peachtree and North Avenue. The building was constructed of granite quarried from Stone Mountain, the largest piece of exposed granite in the world. It was contributed by Samuel H. and William H. Venable, owners of the mountain.

The William B. Lowe home, located two houses south of the new church, was the scene of an elaborate wedding near the turn of the century when Miss Rebie Lowe became the bride of James W. English, Jr. The house was one of Atlanta's finest and it was among the first to have furnace heat and gas chandeliers. Its spacious rooms were appointed with "superb modern furniture" which was in sharp contrast to the heavy, dark furniture typical of the Victorian Era. The handsome parlor with its silk-tapestried walls and bird's-eye maple furniture was the scene of many a ball, party, and reception.

Another important wedding of the period united Miss Lucy Cook Peel and William H. Kiser. The vows were said at the Peachtree residence of the bride's parents, Colonel and and Mrs. William Lawson Peel, and were heard by a fashionable assemblage of Atlanta society. The bride was gowned in white Duchess satin with a three-yard train and wore her great-grandmother's earrings and a diadem of pearls and diamonds. The newlyweds enjoyed a European honeymoon.

A third marriage, far quieter than the two already mentioned, was that of Mrs. Sarah Grant Jackson and John M. Slaton, which occurred at the Peachtree home of the bride's parents, Mr. and Mrs. William D. Grant. The nuptial attracted wide and sympathetic interest because of the prominence of the contracting parties and because of a tragedy which had shaken Atlanta's business and social circles five years earlier.

The bride had previously been married to Thomas Cobb Jackson, brilliant young attorney and scion of two prominent Georgia families. When a close friend of his had absconded after embezzling a large sum of money from the bank with which both were connected, young Jackson committed suicide while sitting in a hack in front of his father's house. The tumult which ensued over the popular socialite's untimely death, and an early and erroneous inference that he too was involved in the embezzlement, created a sensation which followed his beautiful young widow through life.

"Sallie Fannie" Jackson lived to enjoy almost fifty years as the wife of John M. Slaton, during which time her character, charm, and kindliness earned for her the love and respect of a wide circle of friends and acquaintances. Mr. Slaton became governor of Georgia and sacrificed his political future by commuting the death sentence of a man convicted of Atlanta's most sensational murder. The Governor said that he acted following receipt of proof of the man's innocence—intelligence which he had learned in such a way that he could not reveal either his evidence or the person whom it implicated. His action was in vain, however, for a mob broke into the prison where Leo Frank was held, kidnapped him, and hanged him for the murder of teen-age Mary Phagan.

CHAPTER
EIGHT

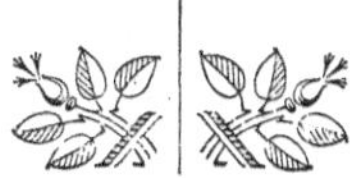

Street of Many Mansions

THE second year of the twentieth century marked the end of the Victorian Era—sixty-four years during many of which the Western World patterned its dress, its houses and furnishings, and its social deportment after the somber style set by the widow of Windsor. Atlanta paused in 1901 to pay its respects to Queen Victoria at a memorial service at the First Methodist Church. A feature of the service was the singing of her favorite hymn, "Lead, Kindly Light," after which eulogies and prayers were offered to the memory of the late ruler of the British Empire. The death of the former Hanoverian princess signaled the advent of a decade of gaiety under fun-loving Edward VII.

With the dawn of a new era Peachtree Street continued to increase in importance and to improve in appearance. The elegant ladies and gentlemen who occupied its great houses were, unknowingly, enjoying the last tranquil years before the motor car would herald the passing of Peachtree's glory as a residential street. Meanwhile, Peachtree and other important streets were paved with brick or with Belgian blocks which eliminated the danger of miring down in red mud, but which also caused vehicles to roll along somewhat bumpily. On streets not paved, treacherous red mud was a menace in winter and the billowing cloud of red dust which followed any vehicle was an inescapable adversary of well-groomed passengers in summer.

Peachtree residents led the city in the ownership of beautiful, dashing, and speedy carriages, carts, wagons, and buckboards. They competed—with slight success—against Colonel Robert Lowry's magnificent tallyho, which continued to delight Atlantians of all ages until the old gentleman finally bowed to the mechanical age and sold his stables.

One of the handsomest conveyances in Atlanta was Colonel W. A. Hemphill's wagonette, a heavy and substantial vehicle with two long seats facing each other behind the driver's seat. Clarence Knowles owned an especially handsome brougham, while Clark Howell had an attractive seaside surrey. McAllen Marsh, one of the city's wealthiest and most popular beaus, drove a dashing T-cart, which was a modified trap. The Frank Blocks' family carriage was one of the most strikingly handsome equipages ever to roll down Peachtree Street. Governor Rufus B. Bullock favored a high platform carriage, and Mrs. Eugene Spalding preferred a cabriolet. The most popular conveyance among Peachtree's matrons was the victoria, which was used with regal dignity by Mrs. Joseph Thompson, Mrs. Walker Inman, Mrs. James H. Porter, Mrs. Henry H. Smith, and Mrs. Joseph Madison High.

In the early years of the twentieth century Atlanta had frequent snowfalls of sufficient depth to make sleighing and sledding a delight, and sometimes almost a necessity. A severe snow and sleet storm paralyzed the city for several days in February, 1905, during which streetcars were halted, schools closed, and electric and telephone services disrupted. Many of the city's largest and finest trees were felled by the heavy coating of ice. The coldest day in Atlanta's entire history, however, was on February 13, 1899, when the thermometer dropped to 8.5 degrees below zero. It brought severe damage to the entire area and caused extensive losses to peach growers throughout Georgia. The heaviest snow on record fell in February, 1895—11.7 inches of breathtaking beauty.

At the first sign of snow Atlantians rushed to bring out their sleds and sleighs. The owners of smart cutters sometimes permitted sleds to be hitched onto them, and the resulting train was a sight to behold. Persons who did not own a sleigh often improvised one by fastening gas pipes, pieces of flat iron, and planks to the axles of the family buggy. It was an exhilarating time, and as some of the steepest hills in the city sloped away from Peachtree, the street resounded with the cries and laughter of merry children and oldsters.

During one of the heaviest snows early in the century a group of young people built a large snow fort at the intersection of Porter Place and Peachtree and Ivy streets. From it poured volley after volley of snowballs which caught the unwary by surprise and which usually resulted in a playful exchange between the stalwarts behind the fort and the passersby. In one memorable exchange Major Livingston Mims, the epitome of civic dignity, was the object of a furious assault. The jovial gentleman, then nearing the end of his life, bent low and scooped up a handful of snow which he rolled into a huge ball and sent crashing into the fort. This was met with cheers and laughter by the red-cheeked defenders of the ice palace.

The first automobiles seen in Atlanta arrived in wooden packing cases early in 1901. The three "horseless carriages" were steam Locomobiles which looked much like motorized buggies. Two wealthy Peachtree residents, Edward H. Inman and John Kiser, were among the first Atlantians to own automobiles. One of the first men to realize the possible commercial opportunities afforded by the novel vehicles was J. W. Goldsmith, member of an old Atlanta family and long a Peachtree resident. When he went into the automobile business in 1907, Peachtree was the only street in the city with smooth pavement and it extended only as far as the Goldsmith home at the northeast corner of Peachtree and Baker streets. Within a year the asphalt pavement was extended to Ponce de Leon Avenue as a concession to automobilists.

In those early years there was many an exciting incident as startled horses bucked, reared, and bolted at sight of the strange contraptions. Inevitably, as the number of machines increased even to only a few dozen there were incidents in which they were involved with horse-drawn vehicles. Probably the first such episode in Atlanta occurred on Peachtree Street on a Saturday afternoon in 1904. James J. Goodrum, a local tobacconist, was driving out Peachtree in his large automobile when he overtook a streetcar at Currier Street. Swerving to the left to pass, he smacked into a surrey in which A. B. Steele was being driven to his office. Mr. Steele, a prominent Atlanta capitalist, lived next door to Mr. Goodrum's future father-in-law, merchant prince J. M. High, on the west side of Peachtree between Linden and North avenues. Both men were shaken and bruised by the accident and the automobile was severely damaged, although the horse which drew the surrey escaped without injury.

Mr. Steele, somewhat amazed that he had escaped with his life, said emphatically that, "I am in favor of a law against this automobile business. . . . A person is really not safe with these amateur automobilists turned loose on the streets."[38]

Within ten days of the unfortunate occurrence City Council passed an ordinance which set the maximum operating speed of automobiles at eight miles per hour within the fire limits and fifteen miles outside, stipulating further that the maximum speed at the approaches to the viaduct connecting Peachtree and Whitehall streets should be "no greater than a walk." The ordinance also provided for licensing of both drivers and vehicles and set maximum fines which might be imposed upon violators. The automobile age was at hand.

By this time the pastoral beauty of Peachtree was a thing of the past. Construction of new buildings continued at a steady pace in the blocks north of Ellis Street, and many of the old houses in that area were taken over for commercial purposes.

In 1903 a fine ten-story hotel was added to the downtown scene when the Piedmont was built by a group of local financiers. It was erected on the site of the old homes of pioneer citizens William Ezzard and Dr. James F. Alexander, on property extending from the northwest corner of Peachtree and Luckie streets back to Forsyth Street. The white bellhops and chambermaids and the excellent dining room at the Piedmont marked a break with the traditional Negro servitors and "Southern cooking" which had long been traditional with Atlanta's best hotels.

In 1903 the First Methodist Church moved from its long-time location at Peachtree, Pryor, and Houston streets to a large granite sanctuary which had been built at the northwest corner of Peachtree and Porter Place.

The former site of the church, upon which Wesley Chapel had once stood, was bought by Asa G. Candler. The Coca-Cola king immediately set about erecting the tallest building in Atlanta—one which would be an asset to the city and a fitting memorial to the man. Three years later when the Candler Building was dedicated Atlantians gaped at its height—an astonishing 17 stories—and marveled at its magnificent proportions and classic detail. On opening day a long line of carriages filled Peachtree and adjacent streets as the curious filed through the marble and terra cotta skyscraper. Every school child in Atlanta seemed to be on hand to ride the elevators to the top floor and then troop excitedly down the stairways.

The lobby of the Candler Building was ornamented by marble busts of the builder's parents and by an elaborate frieze containing likenesses of such distinguished Georgians as General John B. Gordon, Joel Chandler Harris, Sidney Lanier, Alexander H. Stephens, Eli Whitney, and others. The façade between the second and third stories was equally elaborate, containing numerous carved panels representing the arts and sciences. The panel on the Peachtree side of the building featured likenesses of Benjamin Franklin, representing statesmanship and philosophy; John Ericsson, representing the power of steam; Cyrus McCormick, agriculture; Ludwig van Beethoven, music; Edwin Austin Abbey, art; Sir Walter Scott, literature; John Quincy Adams Ward, sculpture; and Sir William Herschel, astronomy.

The Candler Building immediately became the first thing civic-minded citizens showed to visitors. Some Atlantians of the period dourly predicted that because it was removed from the main business district it would soon become a white elephant. But as though in vindication of its builder's foresight and his belief in his adopted city, the business district was soon extended out Peachtree.

Atlanta Masons began construction of a $250,000 Temple in 1907, the site being Willis Peck's old home place at the northwest corner of Peachtree and Cain streets. An interesting feature of the structure was a piece of limestone which Atlanta newspaperman Fred L. Seely had brought from King Solomon's quarry at Jerusalem. When the Masonic Temple was dedicated in 1909 with a solemn convocation of the Grand Lodge of Georgia it was confidently predicted that the solid bulk of the seven-story building would endure for centuries.

The block to the north of the Temple acquired a handsome new structure a short time later when the Capital City Club erected a fine new clubhouse on the former site of Mrs. Mary E. Duncan's little cottage. The club's former quarters in the old John H. James mansion at Peachtree and Ellis streets had become inadequate for the expanding social organization. During the presidency of John W. Grant, son of W. D. Grant, the club opened its new home with an informal reception at which visitors were taken on a tour from the grill to the roof garden.

While these changes were taking place at the southern, or downtown, end of Peachtree, the building of beautiful new houses continued at the northern extremity of the thoroughfare. The first decade of the twentieth century witnessed the erection of several notable residences between Piedmont Place (Thirteenth Street) and the Collier, Silvey, and English farms near Brookwood.

The east side of Peachtree just south of Fourteenth Street was the site chosen by Fleming Grantland duBignon for his two-story yellow brick house with classic Corinthian columns. Across the street William A. Wimbish constructed a stone house patterned after a French chateau which his wife had admired in the course of extensive European travel. The slightly elevated property on the east side of Peachtree between Fourteenth and Fifteenth streets was crowned by the noble white-columned mansion, "Hillcrest," home of banker John E. Murphy. Set in a sweeping expanse of emerald green lawn, the stately house added a dignity and beauty to Peachtree such as the thoroughfare had not known since commerce began to encroach upon the Leyden house.

Elegantly appointed throughout with fine furnishings and *objets d'art*, the Murphy home was especially noted for its lovely Louis XV drawing room. Its walls were paneled in rose tapestry and the draperies of soft rose velvet embroidered with gold had been made by nuns in a French convent. The ceiling of French gray and gold leaf was the work of Italian artisans who had spent eighteen months carving and painting the interior walls and ceilings of the house. A beautiful marble mantel, a rare crystal chandelier, and a choice collection of period furniture and *bric-a-brac* were outstanding features of the drawing room. There, as throughout the house, the floor was covered by a rug which had been hand made in Austria to carry out the color scheme of the room.

The third floor of "Hillcrest" was devoted to a huge, handsomely decorated ballroom, the scene of many gay balls and parties. The Murphys were noted for their lavish hospitality and the annual Christmas parties which they gave. Mrs. Murphy expected her guests to arrive promptly at eight o'clock, and usually dancing, games, and conversation were enjoyed until a light breakfast was served at dawn. The horses which in the early years stood in the frosty air awaiting the departure of their owners were always provided with blankets in the event the drivers had not brought their own.

As a result of an important real estate transaction in 1904, Mr. and Mrs. Murphy soon had dozens of new neighbors ensconced in attractive new houses to the north of their property. This resulted from the sale of the southernmost of three land lots which had been owned by pioneer citizen George Washington Collier. The boundaries of the property sold by the administrators of Mr. Collier's estate extended from West Peachtree Street east between Fourteenth and Fifteenth streets and the Murphy property to Piedmont Avenue, thence to Montgomery Ferry Drive and west to what is now Rhodes Center, and, finally, south along West Peachtree almost to Fourteenth Street. Mr. Collier had bought the entire 202½ acres in 1847 for the sum of $150; its sale in 1904 brought $300,000.

This portion of the Collier domain was bought by a group of local investors who subdivided it and made a substantial profit on the sale of choice residential lots. Known originally as Peachtree Garden, the area was renamed Ansley Park after financier Edwin P. Ansley acquired sole control and spent a million dollars in developing it.

One of the few lots on Peachtree between Fifteenth Street and Peachtree Circle which was not included in the sale was the property at the northwest corner of Fifteenth. It was owned by Dr. Floyd W. McRae, whose wife was a niece of Wash Collier, and who had built for his family an attractive two-story house on the hillside overlooking the soon-to-be fashionable residential section.

Midway in the same block a two-story house with classic proportions and stately columns was constructed of cream-colored brick for Edgar Poe McBurney. The owner was president of the Empire Cotton Mills and was prominently identified with other business and civic undertakings. Although old Atlantians mentioned with pursed lips that his father had been a "Yankee informer" while living in Macon during the Civil War, the son was highly regarded. Beautiful gardens were designed at the Peachtree Street house under the skillful direction of the second Mrs. McBurney, and soon "Villa Nelili" was one of the showplaces of Atlanta.

On the property to the south of the McBurney residence Mell R. Wilkinson built a spacious two-story house of stone and brick. Of no great architectural distinction, it was nonetheless an imposing addition to the Peachtree scene. Mr. Wilkinson had for some years been associated with his father-in-law, Edward K. Van Winkle, in the Van Winkle Gin and Machinery Company. He chose the site of his new home because of his close friendship with Edgar Poe McBurney, whom he had come to know while both were Bell House boys. Mrs. Wilkinson and the queenly second wife of Mr. McBurney were both natives of Paterson, New Jersey.

An interesting addition to Atlanta's fashionable residential section in this period was a stone mansion which was built on the west side of Peachtree, facing newly-opened Peachtree Circle. Its owner was A. G. Rhodes, who as a poor young Kentucky farm boy had come to Atlanta after the Civil War and earned a sizable fortune through the operation of a chain of medium-price furniture stores. While enjoying a leisurely boat trip down the Rhine River in the course of a European journey, Mr. Rhodes had seen an old castle which struck his fancy. Upon returning to Atlanta he commissioned an architect to duplicate it in miniature and soon set about building it on his part of the old Collier farm. The turreted mansion was built entirely of Stone Mountain granite.

One of the most remarkable features of "La Reve," as the house was called, was a series of beautiful stained glass windows in the stairwell. Made by the famous New York firm of Tiffany & Company at a cost of $40,000, the windows depicted civil and military leaders of the Confederacy, Civil War battle scenes, and official seals of those states which comprised the Confederate States of America. One scene showed a fine ante-bellum house set amid fields of white cotton; a companion scene showed the aging master returning from the war to find his home decaying and his fields overgrown with weeds. All of the windows were done in beautiful colors, and when the sun was shining the view of them was memorable.

The grandest house ever to grace Peachtree Street had been erected a few years earlier almost a mile beyond the Rhodes home, in an area then devoted to the farms of Captain J. W. English, John Silvey, and others. It was built for Colonel Clifford L. Anderson, a distinguished attorney and state legislator who was a founder of the Trust Company of Georgia. Set far back from the street on a slight knoll in the center of a lot which fronted 300 feet on Peachtree, the house commanded a breathtaking view of the wooded hills and valleys north of Atlanta. Its great two-story bulk was softened and graced by a gently curving colonnade of fourteen Corinthian columns. Another ten of the magnificent pillars were visible at the east side of the house, where they surrounded a large piazza. The airy and stately beauty of Colonel Anderson's white house was the epitome of the Old South, although it dated some 30 years from the end of the great sectional conflict which ended that way of life.

In 1912 "La Collina," as the Andersons had named the beautiful estate, was purchased by Washington Seminary and from that time forward it was "home" to three generations of proper young ladies. The Seminary had been established in 1878 in the West Peachtree Street residence of General and Mrs. W. S. Walker. Its founders were the Misses Anita and Lola Washington, grand-nieces of George Washington. From its earliest days Washington Seminary tactfully avoided such words as "select" and "exclusive," but it was without question "fashionable" from its first day to its last.

Across Peachtree and some 200 feet nearer the city a brick and stone mansion was moved in 1903 from its former location at the southeast corner of Spring and Marietta streets. The ornate Romanesque Revival structure had been built in 1887 for pioneer merchant John Silvey. Its original site had previously been occupied by the home of his father, Drury Silvey, and members of Sherman's staff were said to have lived there during the occupation of Atlanta in 1864. When John Silvey decided to build a new house he determined to put it at the same location so that he would continue to be near his wholesale dry goods business, which was then located on Decatur Street a few feet from Peachtree. Later he realized that business would soon overtake all of Marietta Street; so he bought a piece of woodland several miles out Peachtree and planned to have the house moved to that site. Death intervened, however, but six years later his only child, Katie (by then Mrs. William A. Speer), carried through Mr. Silvey's plan. Each brick, stone, and board in the house was carefully numbered as the house was dismantled, and reconstruction proceeded without a hitch.

The twenty-room Speer mansion was a decided asset to Peachtree Street. Its towers, turrets, chimneys, porches, dormer windows, bay windows, and carriage porch as seen through a frame of handsome old oaks reminded Atlantians of a venerable French chateau. The grounds were beautifully

Courtesy Atlanta Historical Society

GEORGIAN TERRACE HOTEL

Courtesy Atlanta Historical Society

THE MURPHY HOME NOW HOUSES AN INSURANCE FIRM

MEN OF PEACHTREE *Courtesy Atlanta Historical Society*
Livingston Mims (top left), Henry W. Grady (top right), Samuel M. Inman (lower left), and William Lawson Peel (lower right)

WOMEN OF PEACHTREE *Courtesy Atlanta Historical Society*

The second Mrs. Livingston Mims (top left), Mrs. William Lawson Peel (top right), the second Mrs. Samuel M. Inman (lower left), and Margaret Mitchell (Mrs. John R.) Marsh (lower right)

RHODES MEMORIAL HALL *Courtesy Atlanta Historical Society*
A. G. Rhodes patterned his home after a Bavarian castle

S. M. INMAN HOME *Courtesy Atlanta Historical Society*
Franklin Simon Store now occupies this site

landscaped and a sunken garden at the rear of the house was a place of exceptional beauty. The front lawn was ornamented by several choice pieces of statuary and by a covey of cement ducks which delighted many childish hearts.

As Peachtree Street grew, flourished, and became more beautiful with each passing year, one of its fashionable figures was Telamon Cruger Cuyler Smith, son of Mr. and Mrs. Henry H. Smith. He lived with his parents in their attractive Peachtree Street residence and was associated with his father in the latter's cotton brokerage firm. A graduate of the University of Georgia, he was a debonair and popular member of Atlanta's gayest social circles. His wife was the former Grace Barton of California, daughter of a gold miner who had struck it rich in '49. The couple had been married at the Waldorf-Astoria Hotel in 1900 before a notable assemblage of New York and Georgia society.

In 1904, shortly after his father's death, Cuyler Smith exploded a bomb which rocked Atlanta social circles from the Capital City Club to the Piedmont Driving Club. He filed a petition in Superior Court which requested permission to change the order of his names so that he might become Telamon Cruger Smith Cuyler. The change was desired, the petition stated, so that the name of his mother's family might be perpetuated. The Cuyler name, which had been distinguished in Georgia since Telamon Cruger Cuyler settled at Savannah in 1768, had become extinct in Georgia and almost so in the United States.

The mere filing of such a petition was in itself unusual; when the petitioner happened to be a nationally known socialite such as Cuyler Smith, the story was front-page news in New York and California as well as in Atlanta. What really created a sensation, however, was the unexpected sequel to the filing of the petition.

When Jasper Smith, who was no relation to Cuyler Smith, read the story in the newspapers he let out a howl of indignation. (This was the same man who had built the unusual "House That Jack Built" at the northwest corner of Peachtree and James streets and who habitually refused to wear a necktie.) "Uncle Jack" burst into print alleging that he had no idea of permitting the younger man to change the arrangement of his names.

"In addition to Reuben Arnold and Hoke Smith," he said in part, "I have employed one of Georgia's brilliant lawyers and silver-tongued orators, Colonel Eb T. Williams, to represent me and six million other Smiths in the United States to help save Telamon Cruger Cuyler Smith from the awful fate and utter oblivion into which he is about to plunge.

"I have cited many of the great men of the Smith family who have won renown in the national councils and Presidents' cabinets. They need no eulogies from me, but I want Cuyler to remain in the family to represent the Smith family in the realm of society and as an authority on shirt waists, what sort of scarfpins to wear and how to ride horseback."

Cuyler, who was in New York when he read of "Uncle Jack's" opposition, replied coldly, "I don't know this man Jack Smith. . . . I think he must be crazy."[39]

The verbal and legal battle lasted almost a year, during which newspaper readers across the country were entertained by the antics of "Uncle Jack" and the haughty disdain of the man he had chosen to protect.

Telamon Cruger Cuyler Smith emerged from the fray triumphant as Telamon Cruger Smith Cuyler. For almost fifty years he continued to be a dashing figure, a *bon vivant* to the last, a raconteur whose tales of "old Atlanta" charmed a younger generation of newspaper readers.

CHAPTER NINE

Violence and Visitors

As Atlanta continued to grow in size and importance the downtown business district took on the appearance of a city. There were still a few trees and residences within four blocks of Five Points, but for the most part commerce had taken over. Always the hub and heart of Atlanta, Five Points was the crossroads of the city—a place where one always encountered friends and where the paths of people from all parts of the state crossed. The artesian well in the middle of the intersection had been condemned by the Board of Health shortly after a new waterworks system on the Chattahoochee River had been put into use late in the nineteenth century, but Five Points remained a favorite spot for greetings and gossip.

The Five Points drug store of Elkin & Watson was invaded by a strange visitor one mild morning in 1906 while a group of "regulars" were sipping their morning coffee. As startled customers dropped their cups and clerks upset bottles of pills, a majestic lion walked in and calmly sat down among the pills and broken bottles. Flicking his tail contentedly, he looked on with mild curiosity as patrons and employees fled the store. Soon the beast's owner rushed in from the nearby Bijou Theater, where he was preparing to present an act, and flung his arms around the noble lion. The two left promptly and casually, apparently oblivious to the stares of hundreds of Atlantians who watched from the safety of nearby stores and offices.

Elkin & Watson acquired competition a year later when

a soda fountain and candy store was opened on the east side of Peachtree near the intersection of Broad and Luckie streets. Its owner was James H. Nunnally, son-in-law of machinery manufacturer and bank president George Winship, and himself manufacturer of a well-known line of candy. Known simply as Nunnally's, the new business quickly became a favorite gathering place for Atlanta's young people. The specialty of the house was brick ice cream with center designs of diamonds, hearts, clubs, spades, slippers, and other engaging patterns. There in the mahogany booths and at the little marble-topped tables among the candy jars many an ardent youth gazed into the eyes of the aloof Gibson Girl seated before him. Modulated laughter and an aura of chaste contentment were the hallmarks of Nunnally's. Soon everyone who was anyone in young Atlanta trekked there for refreshment after the theater and for a *tête-à-tête* in mid-afternoon.

In those years the burly policemen who afforded protection against lawlessness patrolled Peachtree and adjoining streets on horseback and bicycle. They wore smart blue uniforms patterned after Confederate Army dress and many of them sported carefully tended mustaches. The policemen assigned to foot patrols devised a code system which they tapped out with their long night sticks. A certain number of raps on the sidewalk meant an officer needed help and another number of raps meant that he wanted to meet another policeman. In the still dark hours a night stick tapping on the pavement could be heard half a dozen blocks away.

The police force faced a severe test on September 22, 1906, and in the three days which followed. The terror which swept Atlanta in those tense days and nights stemmed partially from a heated gubernatorial contest which had ended a month earlier. Atlanta attorney Hoke Smith was the victor, riding into office on a campaign which advocated a constitutional amendment to disfranchise the Negro. The passions aroused by the campaign were further stimulated by local newspapers in their sensational reporting of repeated assaults by Negroes upon white women. On the night of September 22, following word-of-mouth spreading of reports of four attempted assaults, a mob of belligerent young white men assembled at Five Points. Most of them were youths between 16 and 20 years of age who had received their week's wages and probably downed a couple of drinks; others were older and recognized trouble makers; some were persons who were simply angered over the repeated assaults of the past year.

The crowd soon numbered 5,000 men bent upon revenge. Sweeping down Decatur Street to "Rusty Row," an ill-kept Negro section stretching some three blocks from Five Points, they broke plate-glass windows, overturned wagons and carriages, and mercilessly attacked every Negro in their path. Moving swiftly to the railroad car shed, the post office, and hotels and restaurants, they beat or killed every colored person who was not sufficiently fleet to escape. Next the mob turned its attention to streetcars, as though infuriated by the sight of Negro men riding in the same conveyance with white women. A south-bound car was stopped at Peachtree and Marietta streets, and the trolley wire pulled so the car could not move. A dozen or so men entered through doors and windows and when the hoodlums abandoned the vehicle to attack other streetcars arriving at Five Points, three Negro men lay dead and one man and three women were crumpled on the floor with serious injuries.

Despite a personal plea from Mayor James Woodward, the desperate efforts of 300 policemen, and thousands of gallons of water sprayed upon it by fire hoses radiating from Five Points, the frenzied mob moved relentlessly through the city. Even the outlying residential districts were unsafe and householders protected their servants only by determinedly facing trespassers with pistols and guns.

Shortly after midnight two fifteen-tap riot calls were rung on the city's big fire bell and soon 600 state militiamen took over the heart of Atlanta. Colonel (later General) Clifford L. Anderson established his headquarters at the site of the old artesian well at the Peachtree-Marietta-Decatur intersection; the mob, having spent its strength and some of its fury, soon dispersed. The sun rose that Sunday morning on a quiet city, but terror filled the hearts of all decent citizens as they wondered what would happen next.

On Monday night several relatively small groups of Negroes held inflammatory meetings at which retaliation was plotted. Police broke them up before the city could be thrown into another horror of lawlessness, but not before one officer was killed and several injured.

On Tuesday a group of leading citizens met at the courthouse to formulate plans for a reconciliation between Atlanta's white and Negro citizens. By then twelve persons had been killed, 70 injured, and hundreds of thousands of dollars worth of damage inflicted upon private property. The tone of the meeting was set by Charles T. Hopkins when he said: "For God's sake, let us be men! Here in one night the reputation of our fair city has been blasted and we are held up to the scorn of the world by the brutal murders committed by a cowardly mob. If we allow this helpless and dependent race to be slaughtered before our eyes, we cannot face God in judgement!"[40]

The meeting resulted in a caustic denunciation of the mob's actions and a plan to defray funeral costs for the dead and medical expenses for the injured. The Reverend Sam Jones, a noted evangelist, visited Negro churches in behalf of the committee and assured their congregations of the sympathy and confidence of Atlanta's white citizens and of their determination to prevent future violence and to punish the guilty.

Peace was restored and the life of the city resumed its normal course. The actions of an irresponsible mob of "toughs" had blackened Atlanta's name before all the world, and the overwhelming majority of its fine people carried with them the remainder of their lives a sense of shame that such a dreadful thing could have happened in their city. The race riot of 1906 was, and is, the darkest blot upon the escutcheon of "The Gate City of the South."

Prohibition, which had lasted but a brief time when it was tried in the 'eighties, returned to Atlanta on the first day of 1908. It resulted in the closing down of more than one hundred retail establishments and some 23 wholesale businesses which had sold beer and whiskey. Most of the saloons were located on Decatur and Peters streets, but Peachtree had one at the corner of Poplar Street, and such concerns as Jacobs Drug Store had whiskey departments.

Across from the Peachtree saloon, on the east side of the street near the junction of Broad Street, the first "electric" theater was opened in 1911. For several years previous to that time performances of three or four unrelated motion picture subjects had been available to anyone who was willing to squander five cents and fifteen minutes to view them. Except for the experimental motion pictures which had been shown at the Exposition of 1895, the first local showing had been at the Grand Opera House on Peachtree shortly after 1900. The feature was "The Black Diamond Express," and to the startled patrons huddled in their seats it appeared that the roaring engine would come right off the screen and crush them. As the brief and simple pictures gradually caught the popular fancy, several theaters were opened around town. Every showing required two operators—one to hold the film and one to wind the projector—as city council had turned down a request for approval of electric motors, ruling that to run the reels any faster would create a fire hazard.

With the opening of the Montgomery Theater at 87 Peachtree patrons were introduced to reasonably comfortable seats and a touch of elegance in the décor. A tuxedo-clad orchestra provided a musical accompaniment for the silent films, and local residents joined out-of-town visitors in marveling at the pace with which Atlanta was keeping abreast of modern advancements. It was at the Montgomery that the first movie magazines in the Southeast were displayed a few years later.

Atlanta's reputation for hospitality was enhanced early in the century by the royal treatment it accorded a series of distinguished guests. The first of these was His Excellency Wu Ting-fang, Chinese Minister to the United States, who arrived to deliver a lecture at the Grand for the benefit of the Carnegie Library. In the course of a two-day visit he impressed his hosts at a Kimball House dinner by casually picking his teeth with a huge quill toothpick, flustered numbers of pretty girls at a reception by commenting appreciatively upon their beauty and their surprising lack of husbands, and in general asking more questions at a faster clip than anyone in Atlanta could remember ever hearing from one person in a comparable length of time. In the course of a reception at the new library which had recently been built a few steps from Peachtree, he commented when a prominent resident of that street was presented to him, "You are the richest woman in town." The gracious lady uncomfortably denied that she was. "Yes, you are," the minister replied; "I remember passing your house yesterday and they told me that the person who lived in that house was the wealthiest in town."[41]

The next visitor of state was less inquisitive than the eminent Chinese. He received an even more splendid welcome. President Theodore Roosevelt arrived on October 20, 1905, following a sentimental visit to his mother's girlhood home at nearby Roswell. He was met at the new Terminal Station by a group of prominent Georgians and, after introductions all around, was escorted to a carriage and driven to Piedmont Park. The procession was headed and followed by military units and bands; it followed Mitchell Street to Whitehall and thence out Whitehall and Peachtree to Fourteenth Street. The streets of the business district were lined with thousands of cheering people, and hundreds of colorful flags fluttered in the breeze. The dynamic "Teddy," his ruddy face alight with pleasure, acknowledged the greetings with cheerful waves of both arms.

At Piedmont Park the President spoke for 45 minutes on the subject of the area's agriculture. Later he was honored at a luncheon at the Piedmont Driving Club, following which he was taken on a drive out Peachtree and to the campus of Georgia Tech. He left that evening by train for a speaking engagement at Jacksonville.

Mrs. Roosevelt, who arrived with her husband but left for Washington at noon, was taken for a drive out Peachtree and was entertained briefly at the Executive Mansion by Governor Joseph M. Terrell's wife. Among a bevy of prominent women who assisted in entertaining the honor guest at the small party were Peachtree residents Mrs. Clifford L. Anderson, Mrs. Nellie Peters Black, Mrs. William D. Ellis, Mrs. Clark Howell, Jr., and Mrs. William Lawson Peel.

A few years later, on January 15, 1909, Theodore Roosevelt's successor, President-Elect William Howard Taft, spent two busy days in Atlanta. He arrived by special train at the old Union Depot car shed and was driven to the Governor's office at the Capitol and thence to his suite at the Piedmont Hotel. This marked the first occasion upon which a guest of the City of Atlanta was driven in an automobile, all previous visitors having been driven through the city's streets in carriages.

Traffic was heavy on Peachtree Street that afternoon as members of the Yale Alumni Association, the Ohio Society, the Atlanta Bar Association, and the Chamber of Commerce arrived for a reception at which Mr. Taft entertained in the hotel's parlors. That evening the corpulent future President was guest of honor at a banquet at the new City Auditorium. Since the main arena of the building had not yet been completed, the affair was held in the smaller convention hall, which thereafter was known as Taft Hall. The genial visitor shared the speaker's platform with Governor Hoke Smith, Mayor Robert F. Maddox, ex-Governor Thomas G. Jones of Alabama, and Toastmaster Asa G. Candler. Later he mingled with the other guests and joined heartily in the singing of "Way Down Upon the Swanee River" and "My Country 'Tis of Thee."

Much local interest attached to the banquet, for the *pièce de résistance* was barbecued 'possum. Hundreds of 'possums had been sent in from all over the state, the largest of which was chosen for the President-Elect. It was brought into the banquet hall in ceremonial fashion by the head waiter, who stalked the length of the center aisle with one hand holding high the tray upon which rested the thirty-pound 'possum surrounded by sweet potatoes. Taft took one taste, and only one, of the so-called typical Georgia dish, before retreating to the gastronomical safety of broiled shad, wild turkey with oyster sauce, roast quail, and other delicacies.

On the following evening, after a day filled with speaking engagements in Atlanta and Athens, Mr. Taft and his wife were honored at a brilliant reception and supper at the Capital City Club. Hosts for the occasion were the club president, Dr. W. S. Elkin, and Mrs. Elkin. The Peachtree matron was gowned in white satin and carried a bouquet of Parma violets and hyacinths. The Tafts were highly successful in arousing good feeling in the course of their visit and it was said that Atlanta surrendered to them socially if not politically.

Little more than two years later Mr. Taft returned to the city briefly to deliver an address to the Southern Commercial Congress. In contrast to the relative informality of his earlier visit, the President of the United States was met with all the pomp and ceremony traditionally attendant upon the man occupying the nation's highest office. His arrival at the Terminal Station was announced by the boom of a cannon and the welcoming roar of thousands of persons assembled in the plaza, after which he was escorted through the city's streets by prominent citizens, marching troops, and military bands.

Also present for the Congress was Ex-President Theodore Roosevelt, who arrived informally with slouch hat in hand and wearing his famous grin. Another guest was Governor Woodrow Wilson of New Jersey. This probably was Wilson's first visit to Atlanta since his brief residence there back in the 'eighties. The President, the Ex-President, and the future President were all guests at the Piedmont Hotel and each was entertained separately at both the Piedmont Driving and Capital City clubs.

The purpose of the Southern Commercial Congress was to bring organization to the Southern business renaissance which had been awakened by Henry W. Grady. It signalled a real desire on the part of progressive leaders to rise above long-cherished sectionalism so that the South might prosper and contribute to the progress of the Union and it pointed the way to industrial development instead of reliance primarily upon agriculture. The same enthusiasm evidenced by Atlanta business and civic leaders in attendance at the congress was already beginning to effect some remarkable changes in their city. New houses were being built, businesses were being expanded, and new industries were being attracted. Atlanta was on the march.

Peachtree played an important role in the advances made in the second decade of the twentieth century, as it had ever since the Civil War. Several striking architectural changes were made in the appearance of the famous street, and old residents began to be apprehensive about the future of their once-quiet and lovely thoroughfare. They wailed that Commerce, "that ogre," was taking over as far out as Ponce de Leon. As a matter of fact the street *was* beginning to present a new vista, but to the enterprising leaders of the period each change was an improvement. They considered Peachtree more appealing than ever before and felt that the fears of residents of the older neighborhoods were not entirely reasonable.

The Peachtree-Ponce de Leon intersection acquired two of Atlanta's most impressive buildings in this period. The first of these, the Georgian Terrace Hotel, was erected on the former site of Major Livingston Mims' house. Its builder was Joseph F. Gatins, brother-in-law and business associate of John E. Murphy. When the doors of the ten-story structure were thrown open in 1911 an estimated 5,000 persons trooped through its beautifully decorated suites and dining rooms and parlors. A Spanish orchestra in native costume provided music for the occasion. It was generally agreed that the owner and management had succeeded in providing, as their advertisements declared, "a Parisian hotel on a noted boulevard in a metropolitan city."

The second handsome addition to Atlanta's skyline was the Ponce de Leon, an 11-story building containing a large number of spacious and luxurious apartments. It was erected at the southeast corner of Peachtree Street and Ponce de Leon Avenue, former site of the W. L. Traynham and H. H. Smith residences. The apartment house was built by a concern headed by Peachtree resident Albert Howell, Jr., and it introduced several features new to Atlanta apartment dwellers: large and tastefully decorated rooms, elevator service, a receptionist and telephone switchboard operator on duty at all times, and a roof garden. Almost immediately the building with the beautiful twin towers and the exquisite decorative detail became Atlanta's first really fashionable apartment house. Its lobby was busy with the comings and goings of stylishly gowned women and impeccably attired men—some young, some old, most of them prominent, and all of them rich.

Plans for the construction of other interesting additions to the Peachtree scene required the demolition of several noted landmarks. In 1913 the stately Leyden house fell victim to progress, shortly after Mrs. Emma Bell had moved her "boys" to a larger house in the block with the new Capital City Club. The twelve hand-carved Ionic columns which had adorned the ante-bellum mansion were rescued by Miss Rosa Woodberry and placed in magnificent array across the front of her new private school on Peachtree Circle.

The old Capital City Club at the northwest corner of Peachtree and Ellis streets, which had been built in 1870 by John H. James as the second of his Peachtree homes, also was demolished in 1913. Its neighbor, the R. H. Richards-B. F. Abbott mansion, came down a few years later. Mrs. Abbott, one of Atlanta's most liberal and public-spirited women, had joined her first husband in the cathedral-like Richards mausoleum at Oakland Cemetery in 1910.

The home of former Congressman Nathaniel J. Hammond, located between the Er Lawshé and Hugh T. Inman residences, was the next landmark to disappear. For years a fountain in the middle of its vast expanse of lawn shaded by magnolia trees had delighted passersby. The business structure subsequently erected in the middle of the block on the west side of Peachtree between Cain and Harris streets never ceased to elicit sighs for the beauty that was no more.

The old Rhode Hill house at the northeast corner of Peachtree and Cain was another familiar landmark which disappeared. It was replaced by a store building, and the original owner's son-in-law, J. Carroll Payne, moved his family into a new brick house at the southwest corner of Peachtree and Fourth streets.

A notable addition to this stretch of Peachtree was the

Winecoff Hotel, which was opened in 1913 at the southwest corner of Peachtree and Ellis streets. Guests at the gala opening admired the mahogany colonial-style furnishings, dined in one of several attractive restaurants, and received as souvenirs of the occasion silver drinking cups in leather cases. The Winecoff management carefully avoided numbering either a floor or any of its rooms "13."

Evidence of the rapidly accelerating valuations placed upon Peachtree property was brought to public attention when the *Atlanta Constitution* reported that the residence of the late Mr. and Mrs. James H. Porter had been sold for $165,000. The two-story house, which had occupied the property at the southwest corner of Peachtree and Porter Place, was soon replaced by a small business structure. The record price for Peachtree acreage in this period probably was established when the old Thomas L. Langston residence, on the east side of Peachtree between Harris and Baker streets, was sold for $1,500 a front foot.

The triangle formed by the downtown junction of Peachtree and West Peachtree streets was in 1912 the center of a controversy which revolved around the proposed removal of the Erskine Memorial Fountain. It was precipitated by the grading of the two streets, which left the fountain stranded above street level. After much argument by both proponents and opponents of the suggested removal, the fountain was dismantled and moved to a new site in Grant Park.

Removal of the fountain from in front of the Neinmeister Hotel cleared the junction for the later much-needed widening of Peachtree Street, but its beauty was sadly missed by Atlantians of all ages. It had been erected in 1895 to honor the memory of Judge John S. Erskine, an Irishman who had served as judge of the United States District Court from 1865 to 1883. The Erskine Memorial Fountain had replaced a marble statue of Senator Benjamin H. Hill, which was moved to the Capitol as a safeguard against weather and vandals.

Within a few years after the First Methodist Church moved to its new building at Peachtree and Porter Place several other major church groups established themselves on Peachtree Street. One of these, St. Luke's Episcopal Church, built a beautiful brick structure on the east side of the street between Alexander and Currier streets after outgrowing its earlier quarters at the northeast corner of Pryor and Houston streets. The new church property had previously been the site of the home of William Henry Smythe, Atlanta postmaster during Reconstruction. Under the benevolent guidance of its rector, the Reverend Carey W. Wilmer, the scope of St. Luke's activities and the size of its membership increased steadily. It had been organized in 1870 at the suggestion of the Bishop of the Diocese of Georgia in an effort to relieve crowded conditions at St. Philip's Church. The latter, organized in 1847, was one of several Atlanta churches which had been saved from Sherman's torch by the intercession of Father Thomas O'Reilly, pastor of the Church of the Immaculate Conception.

Several blocks to the north of St. Luke's, a handsome granite sanctuary was built for St. Mark Methodist Church at the southeast corner of Peachtree and Fifth streets. Organized in the 1870's as a mission of old Wesley Chapel, it had been known successively as Sixth Methodist and Merritts Avenue Methodist.

In 1906 the First Baptist Church sold its valuable mid-town property at the northwest corner of Walton and Forsyth streets and moved to a new site at the southeast corner of Peachtree and Cain streets, where it occupied a granite structure designed along Norman Gothic lines. Organized in 1848, the First Baptist rapidly acquired the largest membership of any church in Atlanta and by virtue of the great appreciation in the value of the property upon which its first two houses of worship were built, it also became one of the most affluent.

A new church for adherents of the Christian Science faith was built in 1913 at the northeast corner of Peachtree and Fifteenth streets. The structure of cream-colored brick is even today one of the handsomest buildings in Atlanta. The columns of its classical façade rise to noble proportions, and the great oaks surrounding it provide an appropriate setting for what is unmistakably an architectural gem.

Christian Science in Atlanta had its inception in 1886, at which time temporary quarters were taken in a small room in a Peachtree office building. The guiding light in the establishment of the organization was Mrs. Livingston Mims, who worked tirelessly until her death to advance the work of Christian Science. She chose the site for the new church and assisted in the selection of architectural plans, but passed on shortly before ground was broken for the tangible evidence of her years of loving labor.

Mrs. Mims, who outlived her husband by seven years, was always an enthusiastic promoter of anything which might help her adopted home. She and Major Mims organized the Shakespeare Society in their home, and in her will she directed that her beautiful jewels be sold and the proceeds used to erect the Sidney Lanier Memorial which now stands in Piedmont Park. A gracious woman, a charming hostess, and a good citizen to the last, Mrs. Mims was in every way a gentlewoman in the old Southern tradition.

An uninformed stranger who happened to be in Atlanta during the first part of May, 1914, might quite reasonably have decided either that he had suddenly taken leave of his senses or that by some strange magic he had been transported to Cairo, Egypt, in the middle of a Ramadan night. The fezzes, flags, and shrieking men which clogged Atlanta's streets on May 10th, 11th, and 12th were no nightmare or mirage; they were but one small aspect of one of the greatest celebrations in Atlanta's history. Nobles of the Mystic Shrine from all over North America assembled in the city on those three days for their annual convention. Never before had so many thousands of visitors been in Atlanta at one time—hotels, rooming houses, and private homes were packed, and more than 150 Pullman cars parked in the Southern Railway's yards were filled with visiting Shriners.

The Potentate of the local Yaarab Temple was Forrest Adair, member of a family long prominent in the city's affairs, who was largely responsible for the success of the drive which resulted in the founding of the Scottish Rite Hospital for Crippled Children. Governor John M. Slaton was another Shriner of note, and in the course of the convention Mrs. Slaton was hostess at an elaborate garden party at her Peachtree Road estate to which all visiting Shriners and their wives were invited.

The crescent, the star, and the scimitar ruled Atlanta during the convention. Dozens of balls, receptions, races, luncheons, dinners, supper parties, and tours provided an opportunity for fellowship. The Shriners made merry, Atlantians made them welcome, and the combination resulted in a festive, convivial holiday.

A parade on May 12th was the highlight of the convention. The line of march was from the Peachtree-Ponce de Leon intersection south to Whitehall, Mitchell, Marietta, Spring, Forsyth, Carnegie Way, and thence to the Lyric Theater, the official Shrine Convention headquarters. The colorful garb and hilarious antics of the Shriners provided the tens of thousands of curb-side viewers with a great spectacle. Peachtree and all major thoroughfares were draped with bunting and decorated with flags of all the 48 states, and the music of many bands filled the air. Yaarab Temple, then in its twenty-fifth year, and all Atlanta took pride in this colorful climax to "Shrine Week."

Early in the next year the main dining room of the Piedmont Hotel was the scene of a little drama which caused raised eyebrows and scathing denunciations, as well as murmurs of admiration along Peachtree and its sister streets. A strapping man beating a helpless woman? No. A waiter insulting a customer? No. A scene of unabashed romanticism? No. A *woman* smoking a cigarette!

As reported in the *Atlanta Journal*, she was ". . . one of those bewitching blondes in a nifty suit and a cute little harem hat. . . . Out of a tiny silver case she extracted a gold-tipped cigarette, struck a match, lighted the cigarette, tossed the match to the floor and calmly blew a ring.

"And she smoked that cigarette to the bitter end and while a hundred eyes watched her in fascinated silence, rose at last, flipped the 'cig' into the ash tray, took her escort's arm and tripped gaily out for all the world as if she hadn't done what had never been done before."[42]

Later in the same year Atlanta celebrated a gigantic Harvest Festival with a two-mile-long parade which attracted many interested shoppers. The floats, men, automobiles, trucks, street wagons, fire-fighting apparatus, bands, and drum and bugle corps were enthusiastically received. When they had passed, a strange appendage appeared: 500 women—marching, riding horses, driving automobiles, and posing on floats. They were members of the Equal Suffrage Party of Georgia, which was composed of dedicated women who were determined to earn for their sex equal rights at the polls. Miss Eleanor Raoul, daughter of Peachtree's recently-deceased William Greene Raoul, was president of the Atlanta branch. In that capacity and also as marshal for the parading women, she rode a white horse in front of the suffragists. The open touring cars in which some of the women rode were garlanded with flowers and bedecked with banners. At the end of the procession was a large white wagon bearing the W.C.T.U. command "Drink Water."

These vigilant women with their tailored suits and purposeful determination were in sharp contrast to the discreet, modestly garbed women of an earlier and gentler era. One can imagine such Peachtree dowagers as Mrs. Hugh T. Inman, Mrs. Clarence Knowles, Mrs. Joseph Kingsberry, and Mrs. William D. Grant peering through their shuttered windows at the shocking spectacle of well-born young women attracting attention to themselves. How times had changed—and how much more they were to change in the next few years!

CHAPTER
TEN

Peachtree's Residential Twilight

ONE of Peachtree's best loved residents, Colonel William Lawson Peel, was a vital force behind the movement which brought to Atlanta the Metropolitan Opera Company and its glittering array of singers. Colonel Peel was a member of the executive committee of the Atlanta Music Festival Association, which was organized in 1909 for the purpose of promoting five concerts in the spring of that year. Ably assisted by such prominent Peachtree figures as Grant Wilkins, John Murphy, Clark Howell, Clifford L. Anderson, and John W. Grant, Colonel Peel succeeded in arranging for three days of musical delight which were enjoyed by some twenty-five thousand persons. The Dresden Philharmonic Orchestra shared top billing with such renowned singers as Geraldine Farrar, Antonio Scotti, and Ricardo Martin.

The instantaneous success of the undertaking prompted the Music Festival Association to consider seriously a suggestion made by Miss Farrar. "Why," she asked, "don't you people have the opera—the Metropolitan Company?" The Association conferred with representatives of the Metropolitan Opera Company, raised the required $40,000 guarantee, and arranged for the new city auditorium to be altered to accommodate productions of grand opera. Finally, on Monday evening, May 2, 1910, the curtain was raised on *Lohengrin* before an enthusiastic assemblage of music lovers from as far away as Baltimore, New Orleans, and Havana. On successive days the company presented *Tosca*, *Aïda*, *Madame Butterfly*, and a double bill consisting of *Hansel und Gretel* and *I Pagliacci.*

Atlanta's first season of grand opera was a smashing success. Gross receipts of $71,030.50 prompted a "Met" official to remark that never before had the company sung to so many people or brought in such a sum of money, despite the fact that six or more performances were given each week during the season in New York. The Met and Atlanta were wedded in a union that would bring mutual pleasure for many years.

The world renowned singers who came to Atlanta that first year were accorded royal treatment. They were wined, dined, and danced by Atlanta's leading figures; the singers reciprocated by singing gratis at the Federal Penitentiary, at local churches, and at private parties. Farrar, Scotti, and Martin were joined that year by Louise Homer, Olive Fremstad, Johanna Gadski, Jane Noria, Carl Jorn, and others. The major attraction, however, was the great Enrico Caruso, who made his first Southern appearances as "Radames" in *Aïda* and as "Canio" in *I Pagliacci.*

Caruso was idolized then and on subsequent visits to Atlanta, and he delighted in rewarding his admirers with unexpected bonuses. Always he sang at the lavish parties which were given in homes and private clubs, and sometimes his volatile Italian enthusiasm erupted in public places. On one such occasion he was strolling along Peachtree Street, swinging his celebrated cane and enjoying the afternoon sunshine, when he met a nursemaid pushing a carriage. Her young charge was screaming lustily and the nurse was at a loss as to how to make the infant stop crying. The portly tenor stopped, chucked the baby under the chin, and began to croon a lullaby. Another lullaby followed, then an aria, then a series of arias. A small crowd gathered and listened appreciatively, but still the baby cried. Caruso finally ended the impromptu concert, shrugged his shoulders, and sauntered away.

One of Caruso's greatest pleasures in Atlanta was sketching amusing caricatures of his friends on the porch of the Georgian Terrace. The hotel quickly became a favorite with the entire Met troupe, and its corridors and dining room resounded with the laughter and foreign accents of many an excitable *artiste.* The outdoor teas given there under a group of striped umbrellas lent an almost Riviera-like air to Peachtree. There Caruso and his colleagues held court, and there it was that the ebullient tenor languished beside the one person in Atlanta who overshadowed him. Mrs. William Lawson Peel, formidable arbiter of Atlanta society and wife of the Music Festival Association's president, was a regular attendant at the teas. Wearing a large plumed hat and seated erect in a straight chair, Mrs. Peel fixed her piercing black eyes upon the assemblage and all quailed before her gaze.

It was during this period that the Peels moved from their house at the northwest corner of Peachtree Street and Merritts Avenue to a house which was built for them near the turreted Peachtree mansion of Mr. and Mrs. William A. Speer. The new Peel residence was an English Tudor-style brick house set upon a hill which commanded a view of what later became the Peachtree-Spring Street intersection. This was one of the last houses to be erected upon Peachtree Street, where a brief flurry of building early in the century foreshadowed its decline as an avenue of imposing residences. Among other memorable houses of this period were the dignified brick structure with granite ornamentation which was erected for Mr. and Mrs. Frank Inman at the southwest corner of Peachtree and Sixteenth streets, the charming green cottage with leaded casement windows which Dr. Bates Block built for his bride next to the southwest corner of Peachtree and Seventeenth streets, and the rambling one-story home of Mr. and Mrs. Charles A. Davis on the opposite side of Peachtree.

Eugene M. Mitchell, a prominent attorney and member of a pioneer Atlanta family, built a white two-story frame house on the east side of Peachtree just north of Seventeenth Street. Here, in 1920, was held the debut party of his only daughter, Margaret, a doll-like Smith College student who was destined to earn international fame as an author some years later.

Mr. Mitchell's nearest neighbors were Mr. and Mrs. William C. Rawson, whose house was located at the northwest corner of Peachtree and Seventeenth streets. The remainder of the block was a beautiful forest through which in autumn one could see the Chattahoochee River in the distance.

Two handsome houses were erected opposite the Speer mansion by Thomas R. Sawtell, an Atlanta banker, and Eugene R. Black, son-in-law of Henry W. Grady and later governor of the Federal Reserve Bank of Atlanta. Both houses were two-story brick structures with imposing columns in front and both were set far back from the street. Across from nearby Washington Seminary was the home of Mr. and Mrs. Troup Howard, which was noted for its lavish appointments and the sumptuousness of the parties at which the owners frequently entertained. Mr. Howard, a native of Macon, had earned a considerable fortune as a cotton merchant in Atlanta and in Liverpool, England.

Henry Grady, Jr.'s white-columned colonial-style home faced the Peachtree-Twenty-fifth Street intersection, and the James H. Nunnally residence graced the northwest corner.

The iron fence surrounding the Nunnally estate had originally enclosed the grounds at the home of Mrs. Nunnally's father, the late George Winship. Next to the Nunnally house, at the southwest corner of Twenty-sixth Street, was the secluded home in which J. Carroll Payne spent his last years. This house, together with the Georgian structure which Dr. Willis B. Jones later built across Peachtree at the southeast corner of Huntington Road, marked the official end of Peachtree Street and the beginning of Peachtree Road.

The stretch of Peachtree from its northern intersection with West Peachtree to the wooded area near Huntington Road was at one time the most beautiful residential area in Atlanta. That it would reign supreme for an even shorter time than had the older blocks of the boulevard was foretold, perhaps, by two occurrences prior to 1920. These were the widening and paving of the street and of its continuation, Peachtree Road, from Brookwood to Buckhead, and the opening of a branch railroad station at Brookwood. The latter, officially named the Southern Railway's Peachtree Station, quickly became known simply as Brookwood Station. It occupied, then as now, a red brick building situated northwest of Washington Seminary.

On April 6, 1917, former Peachtree resident Woodrow Wilson signed a declaration of war against Germany and almost overnight the pulse of the nation quickened as the United States girded itself for mortal combat in foreign lands.

The impact of the war was felt immediately in Atlanta, for the Army was then at work upon a military training camp at a site about a mile east of Peachtree Road at its northern terminus near the village of Chamblee. It was named Camp Gordon in honor of Georgia's Civil War leader, postwar governor, and United States senator. The new six-million dollar facility was not completed until Christmas, but it received its first consignment of troops in September and for the duration of the war Peachtree and other streets were crowded with young men wearing olive-drab uniforms and leather leggings. As the *Atlanta Journal* commented, "Atlanta has had one or two white Christmases, many green and red Christmases, but it remained for the year 1917 to bring . . . a khaki Christmas."[43]

Atlanta's young men swamped local Army and Navy recruiting offices with applications for military duty. They left the city in droves, destined for training camps and, in many cases, eventual service in France. One young Atlantian was so afraid of missing his early morning train to Macon and Camp Wheeler that he pitched his tent in the middle of Five Points and there he and a comrade spent the night. The conscientious youth was Hooper Alexander, Jr., then a member of the old 5th Georgia Regiment and later a successful Atlanta businessman.

Six weeks after the start of the war a tall steel flagpole was raised next to the traffic control tower in the middle of Five Points, and from that time forward a large American flag fluttered at the site of the old artesian well. The flagpole was dedicated by Major General Leonard Wood, chief of staff of the Army and formerly a student at Georgia Tech, who had selected the site upon which Camp Gordon was built. Preceding the dedicatory ceremony a military parade had moved along Peachtree from the Baker Street intersection to the site of the ceremony and thence to Mitchell Street. The smartly stepping men of the Army, the National Guard, and the Governor's Horse Guards were followed by cadets from Georgia Military Academy, brilliantly garbed Shriners, Boy Scouts, students from local high schools, and Red Cross women. A prominent position in the colorful parade was assigned to the Georgia Tech student body, which turned out *en masse* to honor the man who had started intercollegiate athletics while at Tech and who had the distinction of being the first "Ramblin' Wreck" ever to cross an Athens goal line of Tech's arch rival, the University of Georgia. As the sound of marching feet and the music of many bands faded into the distance, most Atlantians could agree with the *Journal* that the parade was "the mightiest demonstration the world war has yet brought forth in the South."

Two days later Atlanta experienced the greatest tragedy to beset it since Union arsonists burned the town in 1864. On Monday, May 21, 1917, four separate fires broke out in various parts of the city, three of which were easily extinguished. The fourth blaze originated on the roof of a Grady Hospital storage house and was confined initially to a stack of burning mattresses. Since the only fire truck not assigned to the other fires had no hose, however, the wind-whipped blaze soon became a major conflagration. It leaped from house to house, from block to block. Soon houses in its path were dynamited, but to no avail; the hungry flames moved onward at incredible speed, destroying fine old houses and the treasures of a lifetime before dazed residents could fully realize what was happening.

Thousands of soldiers descended upon the scene to help fight the fire, to assist the homeless, and to prevent looting of houses abandoned by terrified occupants. Peachtree and Ponce de Leon Avenue were clogged with frightened residents of the two thoroughfares who were desperately trying to save a few possessions before their houses would also be destroyed.

A heavy pall of smoke was whipped over the city; the homeless wandered its streets in bewilderment; the sound of dynamiting filled the air with ear-splitting reverberations. Sirens wailed endlessly as fire trucks roared down Peachtree from East Point, Newnan, Marietta, Macon, and Griffin. By Tuesday equipment had arrived from Knoxville, Chattanooga, Rome, Jacksonville, Greenville, Augusta, Savannah, and other cities.

On Tuesday as a shocked city beheld its wounds when finally the fire was largely extinguished the terrible cost was counted: 300 acres laid waste; 10,000 persons homeless; property loss of nearly $6,000,000; and, surprisingly enough, only one person dead as a result of the holocaust. A two-mile stretch east of Peachtree extending almost from Decatur Street to Piedmont Park was leveled; the rubble smouldered for a week.

As the sad task of rebuilding once-beautiful neighborhoods along Jackson Street (now Parkway and Charles Allen drives) and Boulevard got under way, the city pushed through a requisition for the first completely motorized fire department in its history. A year to the day after the "big fire" was conquered the horse-drawn fire wagon disappeared forever from Atlanta's streets. A parade down Broad, Mitchell, Whitehall, and Peachtree streets introduced fourteen gleaming red fire trucks with yellow wheels and shining lanterns. These trucks were the forerunners of even better equipment which would gradually make Atlanta relatively safe from fire hazards—or so the city fathers hoped.

The Peachtree site of the old National Hotel was graced by an unusual new building when the Peachtree Arcade was opened in 1917. It was built where pioneer citizen Patrick Connally's house had stood when Atlanta was a struggling railroad terminus. In the years since then the property had increased in value and importance, but it still remained in the possession of Mr. Connally's descendants. The interior of the Arcade, a multi-storied structure which extended from Peachtree to Broad Street, was lined with small shops at the basement and first and second floor levels, and parts of the upper levels were devoted to offices. The tri-level courtyard with a fountain was a conversation piece in the days of the "flapper."

When an armistice between Germany and the Allies was signed on November 11, 1918, the end of the First World War was jubilantly celebrated in Atlanta. Schools dismissed their pupils, factories released their workers, and government offices closed early. Boy Scouts and the Tech High School student body paraded down Peachtree with flags flying and bugles blaring. It was a day of wild enthusiasm and heartfelt thanks that the terrible war had come to an end.

The real victory celebration came next day when by order of Mayor Asa G. Candler all city offices were closed and most businesses shut their doors. Atlanta's penchant for parades was never more evident than on that mild and cloudless day. More than 10,000 troops and many thousands of civilians marched in a parade which traversed Peachtree Street to a reviewing stand at Five Points. Flags of all the allied nations fluttered from office buildings along the route, confetti rained upon the marchers and an unending crescendo of noise arose from bands, voices, and instruments of all kinds. To cap it all, "two great airplanes [from Souther Field at Americus] dipped and soared, looping the loop and cutting all sorts of eccentric evolutions amid the frantic cheers of the watching crowds."[44] It was a magnificent expression of unbounded joy that peace had returned to a weary world.

General of the Armies John J. Pershing, who had led the American Expeditionary Force to victory, was accorded a signal honor on December 3, 1918, when the name of the triangular plot at the northern intersection of Peachtree and West Peachtree streets was changed from Goldsboro Park to Pershing Point. Two years later the War Mothers of Fulton County dedicated there a granite bench upon which were carved the names of the great battles of World War I.

The first non-residential encroachment upon the stretch of Peachtree north of the Christian Science Church at Fifteenth Street was a new house of worship for the First Presbyterian Church. The magnificent structure dedicated in 1919 was a far cry, indeed, from the simple wooden building at Peachtree and Houston streets in which Atlanta's first Presbyterian church had been organized in 1848. The Presbyterians had for many years occupied a building away from Peachtree, but, like most of the religious bodies which had been organized in old Wesley Chapel, they finally returned to the fashionable avenue which had succeeded the dusty wagon trail of long ago.

The Presbyterian Church's new sanctuary and the fine stained glass windows which adorned it were a harmonious addition to the stately Peachtree scene. Edgar Poe McBurney, whose home was but a few feet distant, gave the church a fifteen-bell carillon in memory of his parents, and the family of the late Charles R. Winship later presented a memorial chapel in memory of their husband and father.

In 1922 the *Atlanta Journal's* radio station, WSB ("Welcome South, Brother"), inaugurated the first regularly broadcast church services in the South when it put Dr. J. Sproyle Lyons on the air from the First Presbyterian Church. A year later listeners who tuned in to WSB on Tuesday evening, June 19, heard the massive tones of an organ burst forth unannounced, while the brilliant assemblage of guests in the Samuel M. Inman residence listened in amazement to music that could not possibly originate in the house but was perfect for the wedding ceremony they were about to witness. Through the ingenuity of WSB engineers the music was relayed from the First Presbyterian Church where Dr. Charles A. Sheldon, Jr., was seated at the great organ. The stringed orchestra at the Inman house blended its music with the organ as marriage vows were spoken by young Hugh T. Inman and Miss Mildred McPheeters Cooper of Philadelphia. The bride and bridegroom were first cousins, and the bride was the namesake of their step-grandmother, Mrs. Samuel M. Inman, in whose home they were married.

In 1923 one of Peachtree's most picturesque landmarks disappeared when the old Executive Mansion at the southwest corner of Peachtree and Cain streets was demolished. It had served the state for fifty-one years, and none could say that the $100,000 paid builder John H. James in 1870 had not been well spent. The ornate old mansion was replaced in

1924 by the fourteen-story Henry Grady Hotel, the Henry Grady Building, and the Red Rock Building.

Franklin M. Garrett captured the mood of the many-windowed Victorian structure when he wrote in *Atlanta and Environs*: "The old Governor's Mansion became symbolic of the era of post-bellum progress in Atlanta. Within its historic walls the destinies of a people were shaped, and in its spacious rooms the beauty and chivalry of two generations graced its floors. At its hospitable table the most distinguished and honored sons of the land feasted, and within its doors some of the most important policies of the State were dictated."[45]

Gradually, almost imperceptibly but steadily and relentlessly, Progress was changing the face of Peachtree. For a while the passing of old landmarks was noted with only casual regret, but before long the northward march of business and commerce elicited oral expressions of grief from old Atlantians.

Among the noted Peachtree residences which disappeared prior to the crash of '29 were the James R. Wylie house between Harris and Baker streets, the Henry W. Grady home near Merritts Avenue, the old George Winship residence at the corner of Third Street, and the Richard Peters house between Fourth and Fifth streets.

The entire Peachtree frontage of the block in which Mr. Peters had built his house was bought by the First Baptist Church as the site for a new and larger sanctuary. Edward C. Peters, son of the builder, transferred the property and $325,000 cash in exchange for the site at Peachtree and Cain upon which the Baptists had so recently built a new house of worship. Mr. Peters later built a store building on the site.

Before the great stone tower of the second First Baptist Church crashed to the ground, the two wrought iron lamp posts which had done sentinel duty at the entrance to the church were rescued by Miss Rosa Woodberry. She installed them at her girls' school on Peachtree Circle, where they joined the Leyden house columns and a charming little fountain from the home of Major Livingston Mims.

The brick church which the Baptists erected on the former Peters property was the largest ever built in Atlanta. The portico featured classic columns in the style of the Old South, but otherwise the building was as modern as tomorrow. The mellow red brick house and the frame barn which had stood on the site for so long were now gone, but most of Richard Peters' great oaks were spared. These noble trees remain to this day, shielders from the hot summer sun and reminders of a man whose vision and character left an indelible imprint upon his adopted city.

The Atlanta Woman's Club, which had flourished mightily in the years since it was organized at the home of Mrs. William B. Lowe, returned to Peachtree in 1920 after some ten years in the former Christian Science Church on Baker Street. In that year it acquired the William A. Wimbish home near the southwest corner of the Fourteenth Street intersection. Mr. and Mrs. Wimbish sold their "dream chateau" for $40,000 and moved to Washington where the astute attorney tried many cases before the Supreme Court of the United States.

A few years later the Woman's Club was divided by a heated controversy which resulted in the creation of two opposing factions within its membership. At the annual election of officers in the spring of 1928 members of a nominating committee presented the name of Mrs. Charles Goodman as their choice for president during the forthcoming year. Mrs. John R. Hornady was nominated from the floor and in the voting which followed she received a large majority of votes, but Mrs. Goodman was announced the winner. The indignant supporters of Mrs. Hornady put a large iron padlock on the door of the president's office and sought legal redress for what they said was a high-handed ignoring of the democratic process. After a series of acrimonious court battles the Supreme Court of Georgia ruled that neither of the women was entitled to the office and that the Woman's Club must hold another election. In January, 1929, the vote of the members conclusively placed Mrs. Hornady in the president's chair. The official records maintained by the now-united clubwomen diplomatically list Mrs. Goodman as president from May, 1928, to January, 1929, and Mrs. Hornady as president for the six months remaining before she was elected to a full one-year term.

In the year in which Mrs. Hornady served the first part of her tenure as president the Woman's Club was the scene of a memorable concert by Elisabeth Rethberg. The world-famed soprano was acclaimed by a discriminating audience for her rich and flawless interpretations of Agatha's air from *Der Freischütz,* Tosca's "Vissi d'Arte," and Marguerite's "Jewel Song." The outstanding feature of the evening's program was, of course, Miss Rethberg's lieder, which included Schubert's "Gretchen am Spinnrad," Strauss's "Serenade," and Brahms's "Wiegenlied." In paying tribute to the artist's superb singing, the *Atlanta Journal's* Frank Daniel wrote that "Miss Rethberg is not only artistically pre-eminent among the sopranos of her time, . . . she is a concert singer of equal importance. Her vocal equipment is complete . . . and it is perfect."[46]

The sites of the ante-bellum homes of pioneer citizens Henry Banks and Joseph Winship were occupied in 1921 by a spacious new theater. Erected by cotton mogul Troup Howard at a cost of $250,000, the Howard (later Paramount), although intended primarily as a movie theater, later became a big time vaudeville showplace. It was one of the first theaters in the country to provide background music for silent pictures, having its own musicians who played music composed especially for whatever film was being shown. The conductor-composer was Enrico Leide, who later became the third husband of Coca-Cola heiress Lucy Candler.

Atlanta's first fatalities in a hotel fire occurred on November 7, 1919, when four men perished in a fire which gutted the Wilson Hotel. One of Atlanta's better known small hotels, the Wilson occupied the top three floors of the old Hunnicutt & Bellingrath Building at the northwest corner of Peachtree and Walton streets. Two years later a new building on the site was opened by George Muse Clothing Company as headquarters for the business which had been started on Whitehall Street in 1879. The one-time Alabama farm boy's faith in Atlanta's future was amply rewarded, and the Peachtree-Walton-Broad store continued to serve the needs of fashion-conscious Georgians even after several branch stores were opened later in the century.

A new President and the man who served as vice-president in his administration were visitors in Atlanta on separate occasions in 1921. The latter, Governor Calvin Coolidge of Vermont, arrived on January 26th for the primary purpose of addressing the Southern Tariff Association on the following day. "Silent Cal" and his wife were guests at the Georgian Terrace.

Nine months later, on October 27th, President Warren G. Harding, Mrs. Harding, and several high-ranking officials visited Atlanta at the invitation of the Chamber of Commerce. The party was met at the Terminal Station by Governor Thomas W. Hardwick; Lee Ashcraft, president of the Chamber; and Peachtree residents Forrest Adair, Mell R. Wilkinson, Clark Howell, and Major John S. Cohen. Following a luncheon at the Druid Hills Golf Club the President was driven down Peachtree to Five Points and thence to the Henry Grady Monument where he made a fervent plea for all Americans to work together to solve their national problems. Peachtree and Five Points were packed with thousands of onlookers who surged after the Presidential car as it moved slowly toward the speaker's stand. Office workers leaned from tall buildings in the heart of Atlanta, and a reporter for the *Atlanta Journal* said the crowd was so dense that persons not standing near the President were unable to hear him.

Two other noted visitors of the 'twenties were Charles A. Lindbergh and Franklin D. Roosevelt. The former spent a day in the city in 1927, five months after becoming the first man to fly non-stop across the Atlantic Ocean. This was not his first visit to Georgia, however, as he had purchased his first airplane at Souther Field, near Americus, a few years earlier, and had started his first cross-country flight from that south Georgia city.

By official proclamation the day of the young hero's visit to Atlanta was "Lindbergh Day." He arrived in the *Spirit of St. Louis* and landed at Candler Field, from whence he was whisked into Atlanta behind a motorcycle escort. A parade formed at the junction of Whitehall and Forsyth streets and moved past thousands of cheering Atlantians to Peachtree and on to Georgia Tech. Colonel Lindbergh made a speech at the Tech stadium in which he appealed for public support of plans then under way to develop intercity passenger and freight service by airplanes. As sidelights to his visit, "Lucky Lindy" placed a wreath on the memorial at Pershing Point and visited veterans at the Veterans Hospital on Peachtree Road. Everywhere he went he was greeted by hordes of enthusiastic admirers.

Governor Roosevelt of New York appeared in 1928 to champion the presidential candidacy of Alfred E. Smith against Herbert Hoover. He spoke to a Democratic rally at the Municipal Auditorium, a rally punctuated by the cheers of supporters and the piercing "Rebel Yell" of Confederate veterans who tottered to their feet as the bands played "Dixie." The distinguished visitor, who had been a part-time resident of Warm Springs since 1924, was honored at a luncheon at the Capital City Club prior to the rally. Peachtree residents Clark Howell and Major John S. Cohen, the latter of whom was editor of the *Atlanta Journal* and a Democratic national committeeman from Georgia, were among the prominent Atlantians who welcomed Franklin D. Roosevelt.

Another in a series of churches on Peachtree was opened in 1928 when the non-sectarian Peachtree Christian Church was dedicated by its pastor, Dr. L. O. Bricker. The magnificent new edifice had become a reality largely through the generosity of Amos G. Rhodes, Dr. Bricker's father-in-law, who died a short time before the church was completed.

Mr. Rhodes' heirs presented the late furniture dealer's 20-room Peachtree mansion to the state for use by the Department of Archives and History. Renamed "Rhodes Memorial Hall," the granite castle-like house was quickly filled with priceless records and mementoes of Georgia's past. It was here a few years later that Miss Ruth Blair, Director of the Archives, discovered a document bearing the signature of

Button Gwinnett, one of Georgia's signers of the Declaration of Independence. As only a few other Gwinnett signatures were known to exist, the discovery was of great importance to historians and the document itself was valuable beyond price.

Continued construction of new business buildings along Peachtree began to make the lower reaches of the street almost solid with offices and stores. The 'twenties saw the erection of the Carlton Hotel for bachelors in the block with the Georgian Terrace, the new Davison-Paxon-Stokes store on the site of the old James and Richards-Abbott houses, the Norris Building on the former Aaron Alexander homesite between Cain and Harris streets, the new J. P. Allen store on the former Rhode Hill corner, and the million-dollar Rhodes-Haverty Building at the northwest corner of James Street.

One of the most unusual and intriguing buildings erected in this period was the mosque of the Ancient Arabic Order of Nobles of the Mystic Shrine, which was built at the northwest corner of Peachtree Street and Ponce de Leon Avenue. The Oriental architecture of the million-dollar Shrine Mosque added a glamorous note to the sedate structures which were its nearest neighbors. The theater portion was especially noteworthy, for not only did it afford a large and luxurious auditorium in which to view motion pictures but also it had a marvelously realistic "sky" with twinkling stars and moving clouds.

The mosque was built on the property formerly occupied by the Peachtree residences of George M. Brown (a son of Civil War Governor Joseph E. Brown) and Willis E. Ragan, and by the Ponce de Leon (originally Kimball Street) residence of entrepreneur H. I. Kimball. The Ragan residence, long noted for the profusion of colorful flowers which grew in its gardens, was presided over in its last days by Colonel Ragan's daughter-in-law, Mrs. James Ragan. The latter was a granddaughter of Green J. Foreacre, for whom the house had been built and who had sold it to Colonel Ragan prior to moving to Ohio.

The 1920's witnessed the erection of several apartment buildings in the two blocks between Sixteenth Street and

WASHINGTON SEMINARY *Courtesy Gaspar-Ware Studio*

Originally the home of Colonel Clifford L. Anderson. Riviera Motel now occupies the land

McBURNEY RESIDENCE *Courtesy Atlanta Historical Society*

Now a home furnishings and costume museum of the Atlanta Art Association

EUGENE M. MITCHELL HOME *Courtesy Atlanta Historical Society*

Here the author of *Gone With The Wind* spent her girlhood

FIRST PRESBYTERIAN CHURCH *Courtesy Atlanta Historical Society*

ATLANTA HISTORICAL SOCIETY *Courtesy Atlanta Historical Society*
Noted architect Neel Reid designed this home for Dr. Willis B. Jones

THE TEMPLE *Courtesy The Hebrew Benevolent Congregation*

ALCOA BUILDING *Courtesy Aluminum Corporation of America*

Now occupies a portion of the former site of the house shown below

SPEER RESIDENCE *Courtesy Carolyn Carter*

Long a Peachtree landmark, it was moved stone by stone from its original site at the southeast corner of Marietta and Spring streets

Pershing Point. Among these were the ten-story Pershing Point Apartments (now Pershing Hotel), Stratford Hall (best known simply as "1410"), and the luxurious nine-story apartment at the northeast corner of Peachtree and Sixteenth streets. The last named building was one of the first elevator-type apartments in Atlanta, and it was equalled in the size of its units and in the beauty of design only by the Ponce de Leon and Biltmore apartments. It was designed by the architectural firm of Hentz, Reid, Adler & Shutze, and was erected upon the former site of Dr. E. G. Ballenger's home.

Across this shady section of Peachtree and half a block south, next to the home of Dr. Floyd W. McRae, was the English Tudor residence of Mrs. Joseph Madison High, widow of one of Atlanta's leading merchants. Mrs. High had long been a vital force in community affairs and was especially interested in the cultural development of the city. In 1926 she gave her home to the Atlanta Art Association as a permanent memorial to her late husband and within a short time the High Museum of Art was established in the spacious rooms of the relatively new mansion.

The Atlanta Art Association had been organized in 1905 by a group of prominent Atlanta women, of whom Mrs. Isaac S. Boyd was the energetic and imaginative leader. The group held exhibits, contests, and lectures at various Peachtree sites before their struggles were rewarded by Mrs. High's munificence. A permanent art school was established at the High Museum in 1927, and in the following year a full-time director was employed.

As the effects of the disastrous Wall Street crash of 1929 rocked the economic life of Atlanta, Peachtree Street was entering its twilight period as a proud and beautiful avenue of private houses. The northward march of commerce was temporarily halted by the depression years, but its inexorable course was clearly evident as the 'twenties passed.

Perhaps no event so clearly pointed up the amazing transformation which had made a crude railroad town into a great metropolis as did the passing in 1926 of Tom Pitts' cigar store and soft drink establishment. Long a popular rendezvous, it occupied the property on the east side of Peachtree between Decatur Street and Edgewood Avenue. There, where Wash Collier had once sold groceries and stamps, a generation of Atlantians had gathered for refreshment and the exchange of gossip. In sadly remarking upon the changes which had prompted the closing of his store, Mr. Pitts said: "Five Points has lost its 'town pump' characteristics. It is no longer a place for people to congregate; it is a place they rush away from. . . . I think the real thing that did it was automobiles, and more automobiles. . . . Hundreds [of persons] used to stop; now thousands pass. . . . In the old days, people used to go 'to town' in the evening. Now they take their cars and ride away from town, and at night Five Points is almost deserted. . . ."[47]

It is fitting that the final curtain of the memorable years 1909-1929 should be rung down by reference to the man whose name figured prominently in the opening paragraphs of this chapter. In a sense, Colonel William Lawson Peel was the personification of the type of man who created, nurtured, and graced the city of Atlanta. He and others like him had come to Atlanta when they were young, unknown, and relatively poor; they had remained to become old, distinguished, and wealthy. They were all men with a strong sense of *noblesse oblige*, but Colonel Peel was the prince of them all.

Following Colonel Peel's death at his apartment in the Georgian Terrace, where he had lived in his widowerhood, the Atlanta Federation of Musicians gathered at Five Points and played Chopin's "Funeral March" in a touching tribute to the father of opera in Atlanta. The *Journal* announced his passing with these words: "The lovable, kindly, ennobled soul of Colonel William Lawson Peel slipped from the realm of those who loved him early Wednesday evening and thousands reflected Thursday on the golden qualities of the life which had passed from their midst. . . ."[48]

CHAPTER
ELEVEN

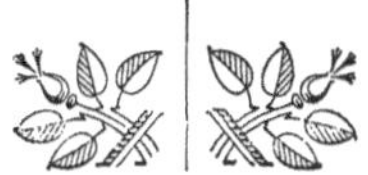

Up from Boarding House Row

THE dark years of the great Depression brought anxiety and suffering to Atlantians, as to people across the nation. The city's officials, its charitable and welfare organizations, and many of its more fortunate residents did what they could to alleviate the distress of those caught in the economic vise. Panhandlers and apple sellers were thick on Peachtree and other traffic arteries. Businesses failed and at one time half the stores on proud Peachtree Street stood vacant. Georgia's teachers were paid in script instead of money. Governor Eugene Talmadge introduced the three-dollar automobile tag. As the state's depleted cotton lands lay idle their tenant and marginal farmers trekked to Atlanta and other cities in search of employment.

In late 1932 Atlanta was host to Governor Franklin D. Roosevelt of New York, the man whose bold and progressive policies were to break the back of the depression. He arrived in the city on October 23rd, just four months before he became President of the United States, and on the following day he paraded through a crowd of 200,000 persons lining Peachtree, West Peachtree, Broad, and Marietta streets. So enthusiastic were the assembled Georgians and their visitors from neighboring states that they broke through the police cordon surrounding Roosevelt's car and forced cancellation of planned ceremonies along the line of march. Later Senator John S. Cohen was host at a luncheon and that evening the

Presidential nominee addressed a capacity crowd at the auditorium.

Mr. Roosevelt lost no time after his inauguration in taking drastic measures to strengthen the nation's economy. His "alphabet" bureaus—NRA, HOLC, WPA, PWA, and others—provided jobs for thousands of persons in Atlanta and its environs, and the city was chosen as the site for the first government-financed slum clearance project in America. The $4,000,000 undertaking was the brainchild of Charles F. Palmer, a capitalist and real estate magnate who was then living in the former Thomas R. Sawtell residence on Peachtree Street. President Roosevelt returned to Atlanta on November 29, 1935, for the dedication of the Techwood Housing Project. A few years later additional units were built on adjacent property and these were named for *Atlanta Constitution* publisher and former Peachtree resident Clark Howell.

The grim years of the early 1930's were not a time for large-scale construction of new buildings, but Peachtree acquired three imposing structures in this period. The first of these was the million-dollar William-Oliver Building, built by the Healey family at the northwest corner of Peachtree and Marietta streets. Named for the two grandsons of Thomas G. Healey, it replaced the three-story Healey building which the pioneer builder had erected many years earlier on the site of Thomas Kile's ante-bellum store. The second interesting addition to the downtown skyline was a new Collier Building, which Wash Collier's heirs erected at the southeast corner of Peachtree and Ellis streets. The completion of the building evoked many a sigh from Atlantians who mourned the passing of the genteel old Aragon Hotel.

One of upper Peachtree's first modern office buildings, the W. W. Orr Doctors' Building, was opened in 1931 at the northwest corner of Peachtree and Pine streets. It was designed especially for physicians and dentists and was considered the ultimate in modern fireproof construction. The site of the building had been occupied in the 'nineties by the residence of Mr. and Mrs. J. Bulow Campbell, and from 1904 the

Marlborough Apartments had been located on the property. The latter was destroyed by a costly fire in 1930.

The Marlborough, the Aragon, and the old Healey Building were among the picturesque reminders of old Atlanta to depart the Peachtree scene in the 'thirties. Another was the Dougherty-Hopkins house at the southeast corner of Peachtree and Baker streets, which was demolished to make way for a gasoline station. Much local interest attached to the leveling of the red-clay hillside upon which the house had stood, for old Dr. Hopkins had once found gold nuggets while digging in his back yard, but no appreciable quantity of gold was discovered when the site was leveled. The three-story Collier Building at Five Points which Wash Collier had built shortly after the Civil War was demolished late in 1936. Farther out Peachtree, at the southeast corner of Forrest Avenue, the Peter Francisco Smith Building also fell victim to progress. The last named structure, a quaint stone building with columns and arches, had formerly been owned by the late Colonel Peter F. Smith, a noted attorney, scholar, and philanthropist.

Peachtree's glory as a fashionable residential street was noticeably dimmed in this period. Many old families moved to newer neighborhoods, leaving their homes to become boarding houses or offices. One exception to this was the John D. Little home at Eighth Street, which was converted into the Elks Aidmore Hospital for crippled children. A large tin tube in which the youngsters could escape from the second floor in the event of fire was an eye-catching addition to the Peachtree scene. A few years after moving to Habersham Road, Mrs. Little lost her husband and then herself died while summering at Baden-Baden, Germany. She left almost a million dollars to the University of Georgia for construction of the magnificent Ilah Dunlap Little Memorial Library.

The economic worries of the 1930's were lifted, momentarily at least, by the accomplishments of an Atlanta man and a local woman who in their separate spheres brought more renown to their home city than any other two individuals in Atlanta's history.

The former of these was Robert Tyre Jones, Jr., who in the span of a single year won the American Amateur, the American Open, the British Amateur, and the British Open golf tournaments. "Bobby," an unassuming young man who forthwith retired from tournament golf, returned to Atlanta on July 14, 1930, to receive a tumultuous reception from his friends and admirers.

Atlanta's tribute to this favorite son began with a colorful parade which originated at Peachtree and Baker streets and terminated at City Hall. The "Emperor of Golf" reviewed the parade from a stand which had been constructed at the Capital City Club. He waved appreciatively as thousands of marchers and dozens of gaily bedecked vehicles passed before him. The crowd which lined Peachtree Street vented its enthusiasm in cheering, tossing confetti, and singing to the music of the smart-stepping bands which were interspersed throughout the long parade. The crowd and the honor guest cheered appreciatively when Negro caddies from the Capital City Country Club appeared with a banner reading: "Welcome Home, Mr. Bob. You Sho' Brought Back the Bacon."[49]

A few years later Atlanta realized with some surprise that once again it had nurtured in its midst a talented young person whose name was to become familiar around the world. Margaret Mitchell, former reporter on the *Atlanta Journal*, emerged in 1936 as author of a thousand-page novel dealing with the Civil War. *Gone With The Wind* was an overnight sensation, bringing wealth and international acclaim to its diminutive author and focusing attention upon Atlanta and its role in the great sectional conflict of the 'sixties. The book was reprinted nine times within a month of its publication, and at the end of six months one million copies had been sold. It was a Book-of-the-Month-Club selection in 1936 and in the following year it brought its author a Pulitzer Prize.

Peachtree had a special claim upon Margaret Mitchell, for it had been the scene of much of her life and labors. Most of her girlhood had been spent in her family's two-story frame house on the east side of Peachtree just north of Seventeenth Street, and she had been educated at Miss Woodberry's School and at Washington Seminary. In 1920 she had been presented to Atlanta society at a reception at the family residence. Two years later she was married at home to Berrien K. Upshaw; the marriage ended in divorce a scant two years later. In 1925 Miss Mitchell became the wife of John R. Marsh, who had been her first husband's best man. At her second marriage the bride was attended by her friend and former *Journal* colleague, Medora Field Perkerson, a Peachtree apartment dweller who later wrote several novels and a charming book on Georgia's historic houses.

Gone With The Wind created great excitement along Peachtree, for the street figured prominently in the story of the trials and tribulations of Scarlett O'Hara. Atlantians delighted in trying to decide which of its decaying Peachtree mansions had been the homes of characters in the novel, but Miss Mitchell flatly denied that she had any particular houses in mind. The author had carefully checked the details of such things as the location of ante-bellum buildings, the weather on certain days, rail schedules, and some ten thousand other bits of minutiae in an effort to make her book completely accurate. Perhaps her only error was in referring to the Peachtree-Whitehall-Marietta-Decatur-Cherokee (Edgewood) intersection as "Five Points," an appellation which was not used until some years after the Civil War.

Atlanta was excited over publication of *Gone With The Wind*, but it lost its head when the motion picture version of the best-seller had its world première at Loew's Grand Theater on the evening of December 15, 1939. On that occasion five giant 800-million candlepower searchlights illumined the façade of "Twelve Oaks" which had been erected in front of the theater. Peachtree and adjacent streets were roped off so that the celebrities who had arrived for the showing could reach the theater without difficulty. As Confederate flags were whipped by the cold winter wind a throng of curious bystanders cheered the stars and other notables who arrived for the première. Each actor and actress was warmly received, but the crowd showed especial enthusiasm for Olivia de Haviland (Melanie Wilkes), Ann Rutherford (Careen

O'Hara), Evelyn Keyes (Suellen O'Hara), Thomas Mitchell (Gerald O'Hara), Laura Hope Crews (Aunt Pittypat), and Ona Munson (Belle Watling). A thunderous ovation greeted Vivian Leigh (Scarlett O'Hara) and Clark Gable (Rhett Butler), but the greatest welcome of all was accorded Margaret Mitchell and her husband. Other dignitaries on hand for the occasion included such national figures as the governors of Georgia, South Carolina, Tennessee, Alabama, and Florida; former Governor James M. Cox, of Ohio; David O. Selznik, producer of the movie; H. S. Latham, Macmillan executive who had "discovered" Miss Mitchell's manuscript; financier John Hay Whitney; and cosmetics manufacturer Elizabeth Arden.

On the day before the première a late afternoon parade along Peachtree Street honored the visitors. It was witnessed by three hundred thousand persons, a number considerably higher than had participated in the Battle of Atlanta. Traffic was at a complete standstill from Five Points to the Georgian Terrace Hotel between 2 P.M. and 6 P.M.; people were standing ten and fifteen deep all along the route to catch a glimpse of the stars. The gigantic parade featured beautiful floats and lovely young socialites attired in costumes of the ante-bellum period, and some fifty bands stationed along the parade route provided martial and old-time music for the occasion. When the stars reached the Georgian Terrace, where most of them stayed, they ascended a platform which had been constructed at the northeast corner of Peachtree and Ponce de Leon Avenue and were introduced to the assembled thousands by Mayor William B. Hartsfield. Later they attended a festive costume ball sponsored by the Junior League of Atlanta.

If Peachtree Street was already nationally famous for its beautiful women and magnificent houses, it soon became known around the world as a result of Margaret Mitchell's famous novel. The book was printed in more than two dozen languages and in Braille and sold more than ten million copies in a period of twenty-five years. The movie, which cost almost five million dollars to produce, was viewed by millions of persons throughout the world and was soon recognized as the richest bonanza in Hollywood history.

A permanent reminder of *Gone With The Wind* was presented to the city by officials of Metro-Goldwyn-Mayer at the time of the première. This was the life-size portrait of Scarlett which Rhett Butler commissioned for their Peachtree mansion. It was done by Helen Carleton, a former Ziegfeld show-girl, and is now owned by the Atlanta Art Association (formerly the High Museum of Art) on Peachtree Street.

Thousands of persons from within a radius of several hundred miles visited Atlanta in the first months of 1940 to view the long and stirring saga of Scarlett O'Hara. Those who arrived late in January encountered unexpected difficulties as a result of one of the heaviest snowfalls in Atlanta's history. The city was crippled for several days as it struggled under 10.3 inches of the beautiful white flakes, but it was only adults who complained; seldom had Atlanta's small fry had so much fun. The city was seriously inconvenienced, but it did not sustain anything like the high losses it had experienced during a five-day ice storm in 1935-1936. On that occasion Atlanta was virtually isolated from the outside world; most of its long distance telephone lines were down, its streets and highways were impassable, and all plane, train, and bus travel to and from the city was discontinued or seriously delayed. The heavy coating of ice made a picture of shimmering beauty, but it caused human suffering, resulted in $2,000,000 damages to public utilities, and ruined many of the city's oldest and stateliest trees.

Something new in the way of shopping facilities had been added to the local scene late in 1937 when Rhodes Center was opened between Spring and Peachtree streets. The $400,000 enterprise was erected by officials of the A. G. Rhodes Estate, Inc., on property surrounding the stone castle of the late furniture store owner. The series of attractive small shops and a luxurious theater were a great convenience to residents of the upper Peachtree and Ansley Park areas.

A new religious body was added to the churches along Peachtree Street late in the 'thirties when the Lutheran Church of the Redeemer moved into a red brick structure on the site of the former Thomas M. Clarke residence, southeast corner of Peachtree and Fourth streets. Previously located on Trinity Avenue, the 54-year-old parish was the first Lutheran body in Atlanta to conduct its services in English. Less than twenty years later the Church of the Redeemer constructed a beautiful new limestone and crab-orchard stone edifice immediately to the north of the original Peachtree church. The clean simplicity of the new building and the beauty of a fine stained glass window in the shape of a cross above its bright red front doors made it an impressive addition to the Peachtree scene.

Atlanta's last great circus parade thrilled thousands of youngsters and the young-in-heart one balmy October day in 1938. For years it had been traditional to have visiting circuses march their animals and vehicles along the city's streets, but the increase in automobile traffic forced the discontinuance of this happy custom. Old-time Atlantians remembered the days when such circus giants as Ringling Brothers and Barnum & Bailey had thrilled an entire city with their strange and wonderful shows.

When the Rollins Brothers Circus closed the book on the annual parades it presented a spectacular finale which would be fondly remembered by the many thousands of persons who viewed it. From the circus grounds on Highland Avenue the parade moved down Edgewood Avenue to Five Points, then out Peachtree to Ponce de Leon and back to the showgrounds. Three bands and several steam calliopes supplied the music for the long line of men and beasts. Flag-waving girls on ponies led the way, and then came horses in their shining trappings, painted clowns, lions and tigers, camels and elephants, a giant hippopotamus, and a cage full of squawking monkeys. The exciting parade with its many floats, tableaus, cages and dens, red and yellow wagons, and distinctive odors and noises filled young hearts with awe and set old hearts quivering with memories of other parades.

In the following year Atlanta was host to many thousands of visitors from all over the world when the Sixth World

Baptist Congress was held in the city. Foreign faces, flags, and attire crowded Peachtree Street as the "messengers" descended upon the Gate City for the largest religious gathering in the history of the South. A mammoth parade from the Capitol to Five Points and thence out Peachtree to Ponce de Leon Avenue and the ball park heralded the opening session of the Congress. Seldom has a more moving spectacle passed along the length of Peachtree: a vast army of dedicated men and women who knew no race, no nationality, no economic creed, but who shared a common belief in the importance of world peace and in the brotherhood of man. With a rousing pageantry which belied their austere reputation, the Baptists moved along Peachtree with banners flying and heads held high. The vast army proceeded to their meeting place to the tune of "Onward, Christian Soldiers," a theme repeated by one band after another. The confidence and dedication of the men and women who participated in the meeting provided a shining example to a world teetering on the precipice of global war.

The rapidly thinning ranks of Atlanta's Confederate veterans continued to participate in local military and patriotic events until the last old warrior had gone to his final rest. The annual Memorial Day exercises always consisted of a parade from Peachtree and Baker streets to the Confederate memorial in Oakland Cemetery. In 1942 a crisis was precipitated by Henry T. Dowling, who was to be Atlanta's last survivor of the C.S.A. and whom the United Confederate Veterans had made an honorary general. The old gentleman indignantly threatened to boycott the exercises in that year because he had learned that, for the first time, the Stars and Stripes were to fly alongside the Stars and Bars at Five Points and the National Anthem was to share honors with "Dixie." The innovation was made in recognition of the United States' recent involvement in World War II. After much persuasion, "General" Dowling finally capitulated and took his accustomed place in the parade. Six years later he made his last public appearance and shortly thereafter he answered the final roll call of the gallant Confederate defenders.

Atlanta never forgot those of its sons who had marched off to the wars which had interrupted the community's life over a period of almost eighty years. Special tribute was always paid to the Doughboys of 1917-1918 on November 11th, the date of the World War I armistice. Parades and speeches marked the annual occasion and the entire city paused at 11:00 A.M. for a moment of silent prayer in memory of those who had fallen in Flanders' fields. The parades along Peachtree Street continued to attract thousands of patriots to cheer the middle-aged veterans of the American Expeditionary Force. In the first Armistice Day ceremonies after the Japanese attack upon Pearl Harbor in 1941, however, the chilled onlookers who clustered around the reviewing stand on the Capital City Club terrace must have recognized the irony in celebrating the end of "the war to end all wars" at a time when American men and women were fighting in various parts of the world.

World War II affected more Atlantians than had any war since the fratricidal conflict of the 'sixties. By V-J Day in August, 1945, scarcely any local home had not been touched by the departure of young relatives for the Pacific or European fighting fronts. During the war years when national defeat or personal tragedy lurked behind each news bulletin, Atlantians bestirred themselves to contribute to the great cause. A group of matrons regularly met at a Peachtree Street site to knit socks and mufflers for the relief of the stalwart men and women who heroically withstood crushing aerial attacks in the Battle of Britain. The leader of this dedicated group of knitters was Mrs. Albert E. Thornton, a wealthy and admired civic and social leader who had once been a Peachtree belle. She was a daughter-in-law of old Colonel Albert E. Thornton, who had died some years earlier following a disastrous fire in his mansion at the corner of Peachtree and Third streets.

One of Peachtree's most celebrated houses was acquired by the American Red Cross in this period when the former William Greene Raoul residence near Sixth Street was turned into a center for bandage rolling and blood donations. The spacious rooms which had for so long resounded with youth and gaiety now became a beehive of activity in behalf of the armed forces. A few years later a new building was erected in front of the old house, but the leaded panes in its third-floor ballroom windows are still visible from the corner of Sixth Street.

Peachtree and other important avenues were crowded with the blue, green, and olive-drab uniforms of sailors, paratroopers, fliers, and Marines. Atlanta opened its heart to these lonely young men about to embark for war and an uncertain future. The Open Door Canteen on Peachtree, and other such enterprises throughout the city, provided a place where servicemen could find a cup of coffee, a comfortable chair, books and games, and a motherly ear into which to pour confidences.

One Christmas Day in these wartime years was bleak and cheerless. Sleet and freezing rain fell during the hours of early morning and by dawn the city was encased in a treacherous coating of ice. Trolleys were hopelessly stalled, and the railroad, bus, and airline terminals were packed with crowds of frustrated travelers whose Christmas trips had been delayed. One dejected young soldier gave up in despair and slowly made his way out ice-shrouded Peachtree Street. Near North Avenue, hearing the majestic tones of an organ emanating from North Avenue Presbyterian Church, he joined a small group of worshippers in the candlelit sanctuary. There he heard a vested choir sing the age-old songs of Christmas and listened as the pastor read the story of the birth of Jesus. Years later the soldier wrote the pastor, Dr. Vernon S. Broyles, Jr., that "I was fighting in a jungle for 18 months—and the only thing that kept me going was the memory of that service."[50]

As victory neared, residents of Peachtree and all the rest of the free world were plunged into mourning by the death of President Franklin D. Roosevelt. The only man to serve four terms as President died suddenly in his Georgia cottage at Warm Springs on April 12, 1945. A prominent Peachtree physician, Dr. James E. Paullin, drove to Warm Springs at more than seventy miles per hour in an effort to save the Chief Executive, but the great man expired before the doctor arrived at the scene. Next day the funeral train bearing the body of the late President passed through Atlanta en route to Washington. As it moved slowly under Peachtree Street at Brookwood Station, thousands of weeping, unbelieving citizens watched as the train moved along the steel rails toward a nation's homage and interment in the rose garden of his ancestral home.

With the return of peace to a war-shattered world, Atlanta welcomed its returning sons and daughters and happily anticipated the time when shirts, suits, stockings, automobiles, and electrical appliances would be readily available at retail outlets. As building materials gradually became plentiful again new houses and business structures sprang up all over the city and soon the face of Atlanta subtly began to change.

Peachtree Street, that stately dowager of one-time elegance, had deteriorated in recent years to a series of rather dowdy boarding house districts. Except in the blocks north of Fourteenth Street the fine old families which had for so long lent distinction to Peachtree had moved to the rolling woodlands between Peachtree Battle Avenue and West Paces Ferry Road.

The 'forties witnessed the demolition of such notable Peachtree houses as the former Walker P. Inman mansion at the northwest corner of Prescott Street, which was replaced by the Jesse Parker Williams Memorial Hospital; the old Dr. A. W. Calhoun residence at the northwest corner of Fifth Street, a large two-story brick house which had occupied the site since 1894 and which gave way to a brick office building; the huge Victorian home of the late "General" Andrew J. West, on the east side of Peachtree facing Peachtree Place, which was replaced by several brick stores; and the three-story mansion of the late Samuel M. Inman at the southwest corner of Peachtree and Ponce de Leon Avenue, which his widow sold in 1945 a few months before her death and upon the site of which Franklin Simon soon built a modernistic store building.

The last house on Peachtree Street proper was acquired in 1946 by the Atlanta Historical Society when that organization purchased the former residence of the late Dr. and Mrs. Willis B. Jones. The stately Georgian home, located at the southeast corner of Peachtree and Huntington Road, had been designed in the early 'twenties by architect Neel Reid. Its beautiful proportions and the perfection of its massive birch-paneled drawing room had always set the Jones home apart as one of Atlanta's most distinguished houses. Under the guidance of Mrs. P. Thornton Marye, a woman of sensitive and autocratic tastes, the rooms of "McElreath Hall" were gradually filled with an interesting assortment of antiques and treasured heirlooms. The formal garden at the rear of the building became a project of the Pine Tree Garden Club, under whose direction it won a series of local, state, and national awards. A delightful relic of "old" Peachtree was added to the garden a few years later when the Society acquired the Italian fountain which had previously graced the front yard lily pool at the William D. Grant home.

The Atlanta Historical Society, organized at the Woman's Club in 1926, in succeeding years grew in membership and steadily increased the size of its collection of old records, pictures, and artifacts. Walter McElreath, a prominent Atlanta attorney, was the organization's first president, and under the terms of his will the Society will some day benefit handsomely. Miss Ruth Blair, former State Archivist, gave some thirty years of devoted service to the Society in her capacity as executive secretary. Following her retirement, at which time she was acclaimed as "Atlanta's Woman of the Year," she was succeeded by Colonel Allen P. Julian, U.S.A. (Ret.), with the title of director. Franklin M. Garrett, a long-time member and three-time president of the Society, achieved distinction in 1954 when his comprehensive history, *Atlanta and Environs*, was published in a handsome limited edition.

The raw, misty morning of December 7, 1946, dawned upon a city stunned with grief. A shocked Atlanta heard with horror of the deaths of 119 persons in a swiftly surging fire at the Winecoff Hotel on Peachtree. The fire had been discovered shortly after 3:30 A.M. and by the time fire fighters arrived a few minutes later the building was a blazing inferno. Inadequate provisions for fire escapes in the "fire resistant" structure caused many guests to be trapped. Many persons leaped screaming to their deaths on the sidewalks below; some suffocated while desperately awaiting rescue, and a few were cremated as they slept. When finally the fire was brought under control a heavy pall of smoke hung over the city for hours. To witnesses of the holocaust it seemed they could never forget the wail of sirens or the piercing screams of persons whose terror caused them to leap from the burning hotel. The gutted, fire-blackened shell of the Winecoff remained a silent reminder of Atlanta's greatest tragedy, until it was rebuilt a few years later and named "Peachtree on Peachtree Hotel." In the meantime, the city and the state both adopted stringent new building safety and fire codes in an effort to prevent another such disaster.

Perhaps nothing so graphically illustrated the changes which were revamping the appearance of Peachtree as did the discontinuance of electric streetcars on a March morning in 1947. On that occasion the last of the clanging, jolting conveyances made the round trip on the rails from the car barn to the corner of Peachtree and Nineteenth streets. Two years later the last streetcar in the city also made its final run, after which many of the old cars were shipped to distant lands. A surprised Atlantian later saw "P'TREE–19th" on the front of an old streetcar while he was stationed in Korea. It was, he wrote back, almost as good as being at home.

Atlanta's electric streetcars had rendered good service since that day in 1891 when they had replaced the old mule-drawn cars. Often called "galloping showcases" in their early days, they had been regarded with apprehension in the era of the lamplighter. Men brave enough to make the charter ride on the first electric streetcar had carefully left their watches with their wives, who wept as bells clanged and the horses used on that occasion reared into the air. How quaint this

EQUAL SUFFRAGE PARADE, 1913 *Courtesy Atlanta Historical Society*
Women in Stevens-Duryea carry signs ridiculing their status

FIRST CHURCH OF CHRIST, SCIENTIST *Courtesy Atlanta Historical Society*
By permission of Steffen Thomas

CANDLER BUILDING *Courtesy Atlanta Historical Society*
The Coca-Cola baron's memorial rises on the site of Wesley

WORLD PREMIERE *Courtesy Atlanta Historical Society*
Of Gone With The Wind was held at the Grand late in 1939.

BANK OF GEORGIA *Courtesy Bank of Georgia*
Thirty-story building at Five Points

FIRST NATIONAL BANK *Courtesy First National Bank*
North Avenue Branch occupies site of former Wilkins cottage

RETAIL CREDIT COMPANY *Courtesy of Retail Credit Company*

YESTERDAY AND TODAY *Courtesy Atlanta Cabana Motor Hotel*

The former Raoul residence (left) contrasts sharply with the modern Cabana Motor Hotel. The Biltmore Hotel is in center background.

all sounded to the knowing, hurried passengers who gratefully sank into the leather seats on Atlanta's new trackless trolleys some fifty years later!

One of America's renowned heroes of World War II, General of the Army Dwight D. Eisenhower, was greeted with shouts and cheers as he paraded slowly down Peachtree Street some two years after the end of the war. To the accompaniment of bands and a shower of ticker tape and confetti the ruddy, smiling general captivated all who saw him. Some four years later he paid another call upon the city, returning that time as the Republican candidate for the Presidency of the United States. Once again, but briefly, he was paraded through the canyons of the financial district and through Five Points. He addressed a huge crowd of admirers in Hurt Park, then quickly departed for the remainder of what proved to be a successful barnstorming tour.

Atlanta's love affair with the Metropolitan Opera Company was renewed in 1947 after a lapse of several years. Except for the war years of 1918, 1941-1946, and the depression years of 1930-1939, the spring season of opera had been a time of wonderful music, fascinating singers, beautifully gowned women, and sumptuous parties since the first season early in the century. For its first post-war performances at the Fox Theater on Peachtree the Met presented *The Marriage of Figaro*, *Madame Butterfly*, and *Aïda*, starring such luminaries as Leonard Warren, Bidu Sayao, Ezio Pinza, Ferruccio Tagliavini, Salvatore Baccoloni, Dorothy Kirsten, and John Brownlee.

Requests for tickets to the Met's performances came from throughout the Southeast and always far exceeded the number of tickets available. In the 'fifties the season was expanded to five operas but still hundreds of music lovers were turned away. Finally, in 1960, the Atlanta Music Festival Association and the Junior League of Atlanta, joint sponsors, announced that the Metropolitan would be in Atlanta for an entire week. The season that year was a smashing success, and even then many persons had to be turned away without tickets. Then, as in the past, disappointed opera fans rushed to claim standing room in the rear of the theater. Atlanta's love of great musical performances and its delight in the excitements of the opera season seemed always to cause a demand for tickets far exceeding the number available.

The city lost one of its most gifted citizens on a hot summer day in 1949 when Margaret Mitchell Marsh died of injuries sustained when struck by a speeding automobile several days earlier. The celebrated author of *Gone With The Wind* had been injured in front of a foreign-movie theater at the northwest corner of Peachtree and Thirteenth streets, just a few blocks from the white-columned house where she had spent her girlhood. Atlanta's grief at the death of the tiny and retiring creator of Scarlett and Rhett was a tribute to her genius as a writer and her qualities as a person. When the funeral cortège crossed Peachtree at Fifth Street en route to Oakland Cemetery, hundreds of grieving admirers lined the curb and others watched from windows and porches. Margaret Mitchell had made the early days of Atlanta and Peachtree so real that readers of her great Civil War novel could feel that they, too, had known the joys and sorrows of the Civil War period.

An historic downtown landmark was destroyed in 1950 when fire ravaged the massive seven-story Masonic Temple at the northwest corner of Peachtree and Cain streets. At the peak of the blaze flames surged through the full height of the building as the wood-frame inner walls and floors crumbled and fell to lower levels, forming a roaring pyre at the base. Subsequently a combination apparel shop and parking garage was erected on the valuable site in the heart of the city's shopping area. Ten years after the fire Atlanta Masons moved into a $1,000,000 building which had been erected on the site of the former McKenzie home at the northwest corner of Peachtree and Deering Road.

The simple act of transferring ownership of an antique lamp post signalled the end of one of Atlanta's most famous institutions. The old lamp was presented to the Atlanta Historical Society in 1951 by the last of the "Bell House Boys" following the official disbandment of that group. One of the original fifty ornamental gas lamps that had been lighted on Christmas Day, 1855, the quaint relic had for years been a fixture at the various Peachtree establishments occupied by the Bell House. The complete unit, consisting of post, lamp, and burner, had been manufactured by the Schofield Iron Works at Macon and sold to the city for the sum of $21. Through the courtesy of the Atlanta Gas Light Company, Atlanta's oldest public utility, the lamp now burns continuously on the lawn of the Historical Society's Peachtree headquarters.

The Bell House had moved from the old Leyden residence to a site near the original Capital City Club several years prior to Mrs. Emma Bell's death. In 1914 the members of the select bachelors' group had incorporated themselves under the name of Bell House. Among their subsequent locations were the former John T. Grant residence at the southwest corner of Peachtree and Pine streets, the entire top floor of the (Cox-) Carlton Hotel, and the old Albert E. Thornton house at the northeast corner of Peachtree and Third streets. In the thirty-five years during which the Bell House outlived its chatelaine, the members carefully preserved the decorum and selectivity which had always been its hallmark. For years the elegant Christmas parties given by the group were among the favorite social activities of Bell House alumni and their wives. When the familiar gas lamp was dimmed for the last time at Peachtree and Third, it seemed to many an old citizen that the last tie to the days of a youthful and gentler era was severed as the flame went out.

Peachtree churches experienced such a tremendous growth in the size of their congregations during the 'forties and 'fifties that many of them undertook ambitious building programs which continued into the 'sixties. The plant of the First Baptist Church was enlarged by the addition of a three-story chapel and educational building, while across Peachtree the St. Mark Methodist Church added a chapel to the south of its original structure. St. Luke's Episcopal Church was augmented by an addition to its parish house, and the First Presbyterian Church acquired an addition to its educational plant. North Avenue Presbyterian Church erected a chapel and addition to its classroom annex on the former site of Mrs. Ellen G. McCabe's house, and at about the same time the church finally acquired a fine bronze bell from the Netherlands which was installed in its long-empty bell tower.

The home of the Hebrew Benevolent Congregation of Atlanta, a brick structure overlooking the Peachtree-Spring Street intersection, was involved in an episode in 1958 which shocked Atlanta. In the pre-dawn chill of a Sunday morning in mid-October some thirty sticks of dynamite were planted against the side of the "Temple's" educational building and set off by unknown vandals. The ensuing blast shattered valuable stained glass windows, wrecked a synagogue office, ripped plaster from walls, and littered the sanctuary with glass and splinters. One of the most intensive police investigations in Atlanta's history sought to identify the terrorists, but no convictions were ever made. Atlantians of all faiths were outraged by the dastardly crime; they could not believe that such violence could have originated in their city. Generously they contributed money to repair the damage and offered their churches to their Jewish friends until the Temple was once again usable.

The decade of the 1950's wrought many changes on Peachtree—changes which transformed a street of fading boarding houses into an avenue of bright and airy office buildings. To make way for these newcomers a majority of the remaining houses which had been the glory of Peachtree were dismantled and moved away. No one could say that in most instances the change was not for the better, yet all who loved Peachtree Street for its earlier beauty felt a sadness at the passing of the fine and stately houses.

Among the Peachtree landmarks which disappeared in this period were the Albert E. Thornton home at the northeast corner of Third and the Henry B. Tompkins-John D. Little house at the northwest corner of Eighth, the sites of which are now parking lots; the English Tudor residence of Frederick M. Scott at the northeast corner of Seventh, which property is now the site of an office building; the former Will Inman house between the Raoul residence and Seventh Street, which was supplanted by a part of the Atlanta Cabana Motel; and the charming frame cottage of Thomas H. Morgan at the head of Peachtree Place, whose site is now occupied by several small stores. Other notable houses demolished were the sedate Charles Conklin home at the northwest corner of Peachtree and Fourteenth, whose tree-shaded site is now occupied by a business structure; the former Frank Inman house at the southwest corner of Sixteenth, which property is now devoted to an office building and the Peachtree Branch of the Atlanta Public Library; the jewel-like cottage of the Bates Blocks next to the southwest corner of Seventeenth, the site of which is presently devoted to an office building of good contemporary style; the Eugene M. Mitchell home in the next block, whose former location is now graced by the 1401 Building; the white-columned Charles J. Haden house at the northeast corner of Peachtree Circle, which site is now occupied by a service station; the last residence of the William Lawson Peels at the head of Spring Street, whose site is used as a private parking lot; the Eugene R. Black and Thomas R. Sawtell-Charles F. Palmer houses, whose property is the site of the home office of the Retail Credit Company; and the white-columned James H. Nunnally-Ward Wight home, whose magnolia-shaded lot at the northwest corner of Twenty-fifth Street is now occupied by two ultra-modern small office buildings.

With the exception of the historic Leyden house in downtown Atlanta, no houses were more genuinely missed by all classes of citizens than were two Peachtree mansions which gave way to progress early in the 'fifties. One of these was the brick residence of Mrs. William A. Speer, which disgorged four floors of historic furnishings and rare mementoes of Marthasville and early Atlanta before it was dismantled a short time prior to the death of its venerable mistress at the age of 97. The towers and turrets of the house which had originally been built on Marietta Street by pioneer John Silvey were replaced by two small office buildings, one of which was built of gold and blue aluminum panels. The other old house whose passing evoked sadness in the hearts of both the lovers of beauty and the mourners for "old Atlanta" was the former Clifford L. Anderson home, whose stately columns had sheltered three generations of Washington Seminary girls. The splendor of this architectural treasure was replaced by the clean simplicity of the sprawling Riviera Motel.

Construction of new buildings along Peachtree proceeded so rapidly in the decade following 1950 that the famed avenue seemed always to have scaffolding and covered wooden walkways somewhere along its length. One of the most prominent of the new buildings was erected at the southeast corner of Peachtree and Baker streets, formerly the site of the Dougherty-Hopkins house. Its twelve-story expanse of glass and blue aluminum porcelain-enameled panels extends the entire block between Peachtree and Ivy and presents an impressive sight to motorists driving north on the two streets. This building, like an equally striking structure at the northwest corner of Peachtree and Seventh streets, is occupied entirely by some of the many United States Government agencies which have moved to and expanded in Atlanta in recent years.

A ten-story branch office for the First National Bank of Atlanta was built at the northeast corner of Peachtree Street and North Avenue, the latter street being simultaneously widened to accommodate the heavy flow of east-west traffic. The new building has a white marble façade which contrasts sharply with the aged brick and stone of the nearby Ponce de Leon Apartments. This all seems far removed from the quiet charm the corner possessed long ago when Mrs. Grant Wilkins' violets provided a lovely carpet between Peachtree and the steps of her little house.

The property at the northwest corner of Peachtree and Third streets where George Winship's spacious red brick house and sunken flower garden were located in earlier years was chosen as the site for a towering apartment building. The Howell House, as it is called, affords several hundred compact apartment units for the convenience of modern cliff dwellers who like to be accessible to shops, theaters, and restaurants.

The former Mell R. Wilkinson residence between the High Museum of Art and the Edgar Poe McBurney home was replaced by a modern red brick building to house the galleries of the Atlanta Art Association. It was designed to accommodate present art treasures, to provide adequate space for future growth, and to meet the rigid specifications required before a gift of thirty Italian Renaissance paintings was made by Samuel H. Kress of New York. These valuable paintings augmented the James Joseph Haverty collection of American paintings, the Ralph K. Uhry memorial print collection, the Henry B. Scott collection, and the fine items in the Memory Lane collection which was established by the second Mrs. Thomas K. Glenn. In 1960 the Art Association bought the small frame house which had been built at Union Point in 1784 by Virginia-born Redman Thornton. Said to be Georgia's finest example of early small-house architecture, the house was moved to Atlanta and rebuilt at the back of the art galleries. Now restored and refurnished with authentic period pieces, it is a charming sight to passers-by on quiet Lombardy Way.

The Art Association also acquired the adjacent Edgar Poe McBurney home, the garden of which was for long an Atlanta showplace. Under the terms of Mr. McBurney's will the home was left to Mrs. McBurney for her lifetime and after her death it was to go to the Art Association for preservation as the McBurney Memorial Museum for silver, furniture, tapestries, and all household effects except paintings. The will further bequeathed to the Art Association the bulk of Mr. McBurney's fortune for the preservation of ". . . my home place known as 1300 Peachtree Street, N.E., Atlanta, Georgia, and the grounds and gardens in connection therewith . . . to maintain such home place . . . as near as possible in its present form. . . ."[51] The McBurney house is today largely a costume museum and its lovely gardens have been supplanted by an unadorned front lawn and a new garden at the rear. Several of the great oaks which once framed the house have been removed along with the shrubbery.

A spectacular hour-and-a-half parade on the night of

September 29, 1954, marked the centennial of Fulton County and thrilled a quarter of a million exuberant onlookers. Moving from the corner of West Peachtree Street and Baltimore Place, units of the parade proceeded to Peachtree and thence to Whitehall Street and Trinity Avenue, and, finally, to the new Fulton County Annex on Central Avenue. Included were thousands of marchers, twenty-eight bands, and eighteen elaborate floats adorned with a bevy of pretty girls. Themes of the floats ranged from Five Points in flames during the burning of Atlanta to a display of elegant costumes of the past one hundred years and an exhibit of Uncle Remus "critters" from the writings of Joel Chandler Harris. The Shriners were present with their midget motorcycles, bucking flivvers, kelly green and mustard "Arabian Nights" costumes, and their dashing mounted patrol. Altogether it was a spectacular way in which to commemorate one hundred years of progress.

Atlanta's increasing sophistication has not diminished the delight with which parades are welcomed. The year 1955 was especially memorable for three great parades which, each in its own way, set a record of one kind or another. The inauguration of Marvin Griffin as Governor brought out forty bands, detachments of National Guardsmen, and floats and marching units sponsored by various civic, fraternal, and school groups. Said to have been one of the longest parades in Atlanta's history, it was reviewed by top state officials from a stand erected at Five Points.

In June the United States Junior Chamber of Commerce held its annual national convention in Atlanta, the highlight of which was the liveliest and wildest parade in the city's history. The "Parade of States" included floats, cars, bands, and marching units from nearly all of the forty-eight states. Confetti rained from office buildings along Peachtree, and horns, sirens, and even a miniature cannon created a terrific din as the parade passed the reviewing stand at the Peachtree-Pryor intersection. The watching throngs were deluged with such souvenirs as silver dollars from Nevada, apples from Washington, corncob pipes from Missouri, canned popcorn and oatmeal from Iowa, hot dogs from Illinois, and strawberry shortcake from

Tennessee. Probably the most welcome of all gifts on that June day were ice shavings from Montana, "the Alps of America." The Jaycees had such a good time in Atlanta that they returned to the city for another national convention in 1961.

The annual Armistice Day observance was replaced on November 11, 1955, by Veterans Day. Atlanta's first tribute to all who had served in the nation's seven major wars since the Revolution began with a parade which started at Peachtree and Baker streets. Included in it were Army, Navy, Marine, and Air Force units and eleven bands with pretty majorettes. Government offices were closed for the day, flags lined Peachtree and other major streets, and red poppies were seen in buttonholes and on handbags all over town. Dr. Blake R. Van Leer, president of Georgia Tech, said in his keynote speech in Hurt Park that, "America's hope for a peaceful and free future lies only in strength."[52]

One of the strangest processions seen in modern Atlanta moved down Peachtree on a hot August morning in 1958. Some sixty citizens from the vicinity of Dahlonega, a small mountain town which long ago had several thriving gold mines, arrived in seven mule-drawn wagons to deliver forty-three ounces of gold to the Governor of Georgia. The trip was occasioned by the current refurbishing of the State Capitol, which inspired the residents of Dahlonega to pan enough gold to gild the dome. The sixty men and women traveling with the wagon train were dressed in old-fashioned clothes and they seemed to be having a wonderful time as they rolled slowly and creakingly along sophisticated Peachtree. Upon reaching the Capitol they presented the Governor the gold which they had brought for gilding the Capitol dome.

Visitors to Atlanta in this period seemed to be especially impressed by several things which had recently been added to the Peachtree scene. One of these was the Southeastern Annual Art Exhibit which was held in front of Davison's department store. Paintings entered in the competition were displayed in the store's front windows while on the sidewalk artists from the Atlanta Art Association sketched and painted.

The annual exhibits created considerable interest and soon Atlantians thought nothing of seeing young men and women wearing berets and smocks sitting at their easels on the busy Peachtree sidewalk.

Another interesting structure added in the mid-'fifties was erected on the slight elevation overlooking Peachtree at the Beverly Road-West Peachtree Street intersection. This was an "ante-bellum" red brick house with eight columns across the front which had been built for WSB Radio and WSB-TV. To the rear was a streamlined functional wing which housed what was then the most modern and efficient broadcasting setup in the world. The new facility adjoined Sherwood Forest, a beautiful residential section which had grown up since the Collier family sold the last of their original farmland late in the 'forties.

The WSB mansion, "White Columns," added a nostalgic elegance to Peachtree, for no authentic ante-bellum houses remained on the famous street. The only colonial-style house likely to be preserved was the former John E. Murphy home near Fourteenth Street, which had been converted into office space by the Piedmont Southern Life Insurance Company. As most other old houses had not been so lucky as to escape destruction, the only houses on Peachtree between Five Points and Sixth Street were the former R. M. Rose house near Prescott Street, which was filled with J. H. Elliott's incredible collection of antiques and other historic items, and the former J. Carroll Payne house at Fourth Street, which had been taken over by an Elks lodge.

As Peachtree assumed the characteristics of a street devoted almost entirely to business it was faced with a daily headache caused by far more cars, buses, and trucks than it could accommodate. The morning and afternoon traffic jams eventually reached the point of chaos, and drivers and passengers sometimes let the blare of horns and the long lines of slow-moving traffic get the better of their gentle Southern manners. City officials had belatedly recognized the development of an impossible situation and, as a result, Atlanta began early in the 'fifties to construct a north-south expressway. Peachtree was severed for several years while bridges were constructed at Brookwood and at Forrest Avenue so that the new four-lane super-street could pass beneath it. The first section of the new traffic artery to be opened followed a route which meandered from the eastern boundary of the Georgia Tech campus on North Avenue to an exit between Brookwood Station and the old Washington Seminary property. It was opened in the mid-'fifties with confident predictions that it would serve Atlanta's needs for many years to come. Peachtree was immediately relieved of thousands of vehicles, but within a few years the rapid growth of the city had clogged not only that thoroughfare but the expressway as well. As the 'sixties began Atlanta was frustrated and perplexed by its staggering traffic problem; meanwhile, the afternoon exodus of commuters was slowed to a snail's pace south of the Peachtree exit.

CHAPTER
TWELVE

Pathway to the Future

ATLANTIANS have come to realize only in the last few years that their city is increasing in size and in importance to an extent undreamed of at the end of World War II. They have welcomed the money and dynamic ideas which newcomers have brought, but most natives seemed for a long time to have a subconscious idea that the Atlanta of a more tranquil era would somehow return and that the growing pains would be miraculously overcome. Yet these same persons repeated with relish a few years ago a rumor that Lloyd's of London had predicted that Atlanta would someday be the world's largest city and that the heart of its business district would be centered at the northern intersection of the Peachtrees.

The phenomenal growth of the Gate City in the relatively short span of seventeen post-war years is nowhere more evident than on Peachtree Street. Towering skyscrapers seemed to spring up overnight to replace business structures which only a few years ago were considered adequate for the city's most important thoroughfare. Already in the 1960's downtown Peachtree has welcomed the shining marble shaft of the twenty-two-story Electric Building at the southwest corner of Baker Street; the $15,000,000 Atlanta Merchandise Mart at the southwest corner of Harris Street, affording one million square feet of floor space for the display of all types of merchandise; and the thirty-story Bank of Georgia building at the southwest corner of Walton Street—the tallest building between Baltimore and New Orleans—whose two-and-one-half-million-candlepower rooftop beacon is visible for twenty-five miles. As the first tenants reserve space in the twenty-four-story Peachtree Towers Apartments at the northwest corner of Baker Street, plans for other sweeping changes in the Peachtree skyline are being made.

For more than one hundred years Peachtree has been the main north-south artery in Georgia's capital city, and in the present century it has become the vital spinal column holding together the vast complex of business, industrial, residential, and suburban areas clustered on the periphery of the central city. It is a winding concrete ribbon whose point of origin near Five Points is a continuation of Whitehall Street, which with its various continuations reaches deep into the southside industrial area. The northern lengths of Peachtree are bordered by some of the handsomest office buildings, churches, and apartments in America. Although Peachtree Street technically ends a few blocks north of Brookwood Station, it continues northward as Peachtree Road. Mile after mile of wide avenue winds through a gently rolling terrain which formerly was devoted to beautiful houses and princely estates but which now is surging with business activity. Near the suburban town of Chamblee the name changes to Peachtree Industrial Boulevard and from that point until its termination at the Buford highway the thoroughfare is devoted to acre after acre of landscaped industrial plants.

Newcomers who stand at the windiest corner in Atlanta and watch the everpresent breeze ruffle the skirts of the chic, pretty women for which the city is famous would find it hard to believe that back in 1883 old banker John H. James sat on his porch at the corner of Peachtree and Ellis streets and recalled the 1850's thus: "The last dwelling house out Peachtree was about one block this side of my present residence. Beyond the Methodist church, Peachtree road looked like a recently cleared new ground, full of stumps and gullies, with a winding narrow way worn out along the center. . . ."[53]

The property which the widow Jane Doss of Jackson County acquired in a land lottery in 1825 and soon sold for twenty-five cents an acre fronts today on the west side of Peachtree for eleven blocks north of the railroad tracks and is worth hundreds of millions of dollars. She and pioneer Hardy Ivy, who owned an equivalent amount of land on the opposite side of the street, would be incredulous if they could see the tall buildings, flashing lights, and motorized vehicles which have taken over their rural acres.

Atlantians of a more recent day also find themselves somewhat out of tune with the times. Men and women who knew Peachtree early in the century are bewildered by the rushing and crowding and are saddened by the sea of strange faces. "Why, it used to be that I could walk along Peachtree and see someone I knew in every block," they say. "Now I can spend a whole morning downtown and not see anyone I know."

The city seems to have been destined from its beginning to achieve greatness. In 1845 John C. Calhoun of South Carolina said that what was needed to develop the economic resources of the South and the West was a good system of railroads between the Mississippi and the Atlantic. The territory between the two bodies of water, he added, afforded extraordinary advantages because the courses of the Tennessee, Alabama, and Cumberland rivers, and the termination of the various chains of the Allegheny Mountains, were such that all railroads must necessarily unite at Atlanta so as to constitute one system of integrated roads.[54] A few years before Calhoun's prophecy Alexander Hamilton Stephens stood at the Southeastern terminus of the Western and Atlantic Railroad and predicted that someday a magnificent inland city would grow up around the spot where he stood.[55]

In the 1890's a writer for *The New England Magazine* said of Atlanta: "It has been called the Gate-City of the South, because it stands at the meeting of the roads that lead down along the mountain sides from the north and up along the river banks from the south, and opens its doors both ways for the inter-communication of the people."[56]

The stranger who walks down Atlanta's Peachtree Street today will be disappointed if he hopes to find the stately white-columned mansions of yesteryear. They are, indeed, gone with the wind. But he will find the more enduring intangible qualities which made the street world famous. Its people are still gracious in the mode of well-bred Southerners through good times and bad, and their interest and pleasure at meeting new friends and old are just as genuine as in the days when life was more leisurely. The beautiful women of Peachtree now live in fashionable apartment houses and wear couturier clothes, or perhaps they merely work on Peachtree and wear smart bargain basement frocks; they may be wealthy descendants of generations of aristocratic forebears, or perhaps they are working girls from humble homes. Whatever their station in life, they add beauty to the scene and give credence to the legends of old Peachtree.

The concrete city of 1962 has few places where peach trees can put forth their delicate blossoms and delight the hurrying throngs, but there are still three tiny expanses of fresh green lawn where one may see the tree which shares its name with one of the world's famous thoroughfares. In Plaza Park near Five Points, in Mayor's Park at Forrest Avenue, and in Pershing Point Park are sturdy peach trees which proudly lift their branches toward the warm Georgia sun. They are a reminder of the gentle beauty of the past and of the magnificent promise of the future which meet in happy union on Peachtree Street, Atlanta.

Notes

1. A. Hollis Edens, "The Founding of Atlanta," *Atlanta Historical Bulletin,* Vol. IV, No. 19 (Oct. 1939), p. 291.
2. *Atlanta Centennial Yearbook,* p. 33.
3. Franklin M. Garrett, *Atlanta and Environs,* I, p. 150.
4. Nellie Peters Black, *Richard Peters: His Ancestors and Descendants,* p. 110.
5. Garrett, *Atlanta and Environs,* I, p. 291.
6. *Ibid.,* p. 249.
7. *Ibid.,* p. 294.
8. *Ibid.,* p. 399.
9. *Ibid.,* pp. 441-42.
10. *Atlanta Journal,* Feb. 23, 1913.
11. Wallace P. Reed, *History of Atlanta, Georgia,* pp. 191-92.
12. Garrett, *Atlanta and Environs,* I, pp. 653-55.
13. Reed, *Atlanta,* p. 207.
14. *Ibid.,* p. 227.
15. Sam W. Small, "My Story of Atlanta," *Atlanta Constitution,* 1928.
16. Garrett, *Atlanta and Environs,* I, p. 850.
17. John Stainback Wilson, *Atlanta As It Is: Being A Sketch Of Its Early Settlers,* p. 11.
18. Garrett, *Atlanta and Environs,* I, 953.
19. Christine Jones in *Atlanta Constitution,* June 24, 1944.
20. Rebecca Franklin, "Publisher Recalls Persimmon Grove When Ponce de Leon Ended Peachtree," *Atlanta Journal-Constitution,* Mar. 25, 1951.
21. *Atlanta Historical Bulletin,* Vol. V, No. 22 (July 1940), pp. 236-37.
22. The late Miss Mildred Cabaniss, conversation with author, 1954.
23. Miss Ruth Blair, then executive secretary of the Atlanta Historical Society, conversation with author, Aug. 8, 1954.
24. Raymond B. Nixon, *Henry W. Grady, Spokesman of the New South,* p. 279; *Atlanta Journal,* Nov. 30, 1893.
25. Walter McElreath, "Jefferson Davis at the Unveiling of the Statue of Benjamin H. Hill," *Atlanta Historical Bulletin,* Vol. I, No. 5 (April 1931), pp. 9-22.
26. Eugene Muse Mitchell, "H. I. Kimball: His Career and Defense," *Atlanta Historical Bulletin,* Vol. III, No. 15 (Oct. 1938), pp. 249-83.
27. Garrett, *Atlanta and Environs,* II, p. 191.
28. Mrs. E. Bates Block, "Atlanta's Most Elaborate Luncheon," *Atlanta Journal,* Sept. 12, 1937.
29. Telemon Cuyler, "Reminiscences," *Atlanta Georgian,* Dec. 28, 1934.
30. Quoted in Mary Raoul Millis, *The Family of Raoul,* p. 125.
31. Cuyler, "Reminiscences," *Atlanta Georgian,* Nov. 11, 20, and Dec. 11, 1934.
32. *Ibid.,* Dec. 14, 1934.
33. Quoted by Willard Neal, "What Tourists Don't See at Tallulah Gorge," *Atlanta Journal-Constitution Magazine.* Oct. 4, 1959.
34. Hugh Park in *Atlanta Journal,* Dec. 25, 1945.
35. *Atlanta Journal,* July 23, 1898.
36. *Ibid.,* Oct. 26, 1899.
37. Elinor Hillyer, "Cupid Raids the

Bell House," *Atlanta Journal Magazine*, Feb. 3, 1929.

38. Garrett, *Atlanta and Environs*, II, p. 461.
39. *Atlanta Georgian*, Nov. 11, 1934.
40. Walter G. Cooper, *Official History of Fulton County*, pp. 825-29.
41. Garrett, *Atlanta and Environs*, II, p. 425.
42. *Ibid.*, p. 662.
43. *Ibid.*, p. 722.
44. *Ibid.*, p. 745.
45. *Ibid.*, p. 835.
46. Frank Daniel in *Atlanta Journal*, Feb. 19, 1929.
47. Elinor Hillyer, "Tom Pitts Tells of Changes at Five Points," *Atlanta Journal Magazine*, Oct. 10, 1926.
48. *Atlanta Journal*, Feb. 3, 1927.
49. *Atlanta Constitution*, Sept. 30, 1930.
50. Celestine Sibley in *Atlanta Journal-Constitution*, Nov. 26, 1959.
51. Will of E. P. McBurney, on file at Ordinary's office, Fulton County Courthouse.
52. Hal Munck in *Atlanta Journal*, Nov. 11, 1955.
53. *Atlanta Journal*, June 16, 1883.
54. Garrett, *Atlanta and Environs*, I, p. 228.
55. *Ibid.*, p. 164.
56. *The New England Magazine* (Boston), Vol. V, No. 3 (Nov. 1891), p. 391.

Bibliography

Atlanta Centennial Yearbook. Atlanta: Franklin Printing Company, 1937. Atlanta City Directories, 1859-1959.

Black, Nellie Peters, *Richard Peters, His Ancestors and Descendants*. Atlanta: Foote & Davies, Inc., 1904

Cooper, Walter G., *Official History of Fulton County*. Atlanta: Walter W. Brown Publishing Company, 1934.

Garrett, Franklin M., *Atlanta and Environs*, 2 vols. New York: Lewis Historical Publishing Company, 1954.

Hitz, Alex, *A History of the Cathedral of St. Philip*. Atlanta: The Conger Printing Company, 1947.

Knight, Lucian Lamar, *Reminiscences of Famous Georgians*, 2 vols. Atlanta: Franklin-Turner Company, 1907-1908.

Memoirs of Georgia, Historical and Biographical, 2 vols. Atlanta: Southern Historical Association, 1895.

Miller, Paul W., *Atlanta, Capital of the South*. New York: Oliver Durrell, Inc., 1949.

Millis, Mary Raoul, *The Family of Raoul*. Atlanta: 1943 (Millis Printing Company, Asheville, N. C.).

Nixon, Raymond B., *Henry W. Grady, Spokesman of The New South*. New York: A. A. Knopf, 1943.

Northen, William J., *Men of Mark in Georgia*, 7 vols. Atlanta: A. B. Caldwell, 1912.

Powell, Arthur G., *I Can Go Home Again*. Chapel Hill: University of North Carolina Press, 1943.

Reed, Wallace P., *History of Atlanta, Georgia*. Syracuse, N. Y.: D. Mason & Company, 1889.

Wilson, John Stainback, *Atlanta As It Is: Being A Sketch Of Its Early Settlers*. New York: Little, Rennie & Company, 1871.

Newspapers

Atlanta Constitution, The
Atlanta Georgian, The
Atlanta Journal, The
Atlanta Journal-Constitution, The
Georgia Major, The
Looking Glass, The
Macon Telegraph, The
New York Times, The

Periodicals

Atlanta Historical Bulletin. Published quarterly in Atlanta by the Atlanta Historical Society.
City Builder. Formerly published monthly by the Atlanta Chamber of Commerce. Discontinued in 1961.
Fortune
Georgia Magazine. Published bi-monthly in Decatur, Georgia.
Georgia Review. Published quarterly in Athens by the University of Georgia.
New England Magazine. Published in Boston, 1884-88, 1889-1917.
The Reviewer.

Miscellaneous Items

Carry On, a pamphlet published by the Women's Overseas Service League at Galesburg, Indiana, February 1938.
Five Points: Historic Houses of Atlanta, a tract by William Stafford Irvine.
Georgia 1800-1900: A Series of Selections from the Georgiana Library of a Private Collector, published by the Atlanta Public Library, 1954.
Industrial Index, published in Atlanta, February 1928.
Phillips C. McDuffie, "Woodrow Wilson - A Georgia Lawyer," paper read at the thirty-first session of the Georgia Bar Association, Tybee Island, Georgia, June 18, 1914. Filed at the Atlanta Historical Society.

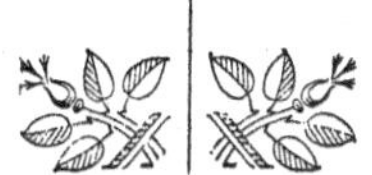

Index

Abbott, Benjamin F., 70-71, 114
Abbott, Mrs. Benjamin F. (formerly Mrs. Richards), 44, 70, 114
Adair, Forrest, 117, 132
Adair, George W., 35, 64
Alexander, Aaron, 14-15, 134
Alexander, Hooper, Jr., 124
Alexander, Dr. James F., 96
Anderson, Clifford L., 101-102, 107, 120, 156
Anderson, Mrs. Clifford L., 111
Andrews, James J., 20-21
Ansley, Edwin P., 100
Anthony, Susan B., 79
Aragon Hotel, 76-77, 86, 89, 138
Ashcraft, Lee, 132
Atheneum Building, 16-17
Atlanta Art Association, 135, 143, 157, 159
Atlanta Chamber of Commerce, 78, 111, 132
Atlanta Historical Society, 149, 152-153
Atlanta Hotel, 17, 53
Atlanta Merchandise Mart, 162
Atlanta Music Festival Association, 120, 122, 151
Atlanta National Bank, 42
Atlanta Peace Jubilee, 85
Atlanta Woman's Club, 130-131, 149
Austell, Alfred, 42, 44

Ballard's Female Institute, 80
Ballenger, Dr. E. G., 135
Bank of Georgia Building, 162
Banks, Henry, 131
Barili, Alfredo, 80
Battle of Atlanta, 22-27, 84, 89, 142
Battle of Peachtree Creek, 23
Bell, Mrs. Emma, 89-91, 114, 153
Bell House, 90-91, 100, 152-153
Black, Eugene R., 123, 155
Black, Mrs. Nellie Peters, 111
Blair, Ruth, 133, 149
Bleckley, Chief Justice Logan E., 36, 59, 63
Block, Dr. Bates, 122
Block, Mrs. E. Bates, 60-62, 122, 155
Block, Frank, 94
Boyd, Mrs. Isaac S. (2nd), 81, 135
Buckhead, 1
Boyleston, Mrs. J. Reid, 47
Bricker, Dr. L. O., 133
Brookwood Station, 123-24, 148, 161
Brown, George M., 134
Brown, Gov. Joseph E., 26, 134
Brown, Perino, 15
Broyles, Dr. Vernon S., Jr., 147
Brumby, Anoldus V., 85
Brumby, Lt. Thomas M., USN, 85-87
Bullock, Gov. Rufus B., 31, 33, 53, 57, 94

Cabaniss, Henry H., 57, 75, 76
Cabaniss, Mildred, 45-46, 76-77
Calhoun, Dr. A. W., 148
Calhoun, Dr. Ezekiel N., 16
Calhoun, Mayor James M., 25, 37-38
Campbell, Mr. and Mrs. J. Bulow, 138
Candler, Asa G., 55, 97, 111, 127
Candler, Lucy, 131

Candler Building, 97
Capital City Club, 44, 46, 61-62, 78, 81, 86, 88, 98, 103, 112, 114, 133, 140, 146, 153
Carlton Hotel, 134
Carroll, Nathan C., 12
Caruso, Enrico, 121-122
Central of Georgia Railroad, 4
Cherokee Block, 15-16, 27
Christian Science Church, 130
Circus, last parade of, 144
Civil War, 19-27
Clarke, Thomas M., 43, 54, 144
Cleveland, Pres. Grover, 56, 59-62, 78
Cobb, Howell, 31, 48
Coca-Cola, 55, 97, 131
Cohen, Major John S., 132, 133, 137
Collier, Charles A., 59
Collier, George Washington, 2-3, 5, 15, 23, 28, 69, 76, 98, 99-100, 136, 138, 139, 160
Collier Building, 15, 138, 139
Colquitt, Alfred H., 37, 47
Concert Hall Building, 16, 20
Conklin, Charles, 155
Connally, Patrick, 5, 20, 28, 126
Coolidge, Pres. Calvin, 132
Cooper, Mildred McPheeters, 128
Cotton States and International Exposition, 78-79
Crisp, Mr. and Mrs. William H., 17, 79
Crusselle, T. G. W., 25, 33
Culpepper, J. W., 67
Cuyler, Telamon, 103-104

Davis, Charles A., Mr. and Mrs., 122
Davis, Jefferson, Pres. of CSA, 19, 51-52
Doss, Jane, 163
Dougherty, Mrs. Daniel, 28
Dowling, David H., 28, 71, 88, 139, 156
Dowling, Henry T., 145
duBignon, Fleming G., 98
DuBose, E. R., 64, 91
Duke, Doris, 66
Duke, Mrs. James B., 66
Duncan, Col. John W., 32
Duncan, Mrs. Mary E. (Fort), 32, 98

Eisenhower, Gen. Dwight D., 151
Electric Building, 162
Elkin, Dr. W. S., 71, 112
Elkin, Mrs. W. S., 112
Ellis, Frank, 84
Ellis, Mrs. William D., 111
English, Capt. James W., 46, 50, 88, 98, 101
English, James W., Jr., 91
Erskine, Judge John, 26, 115
Evans, Rev. Clement A. (formerly Brig. Gen., CSA), 51, 83, 84
Evans, Rev. William H., 9
Executive Mansion, 33-34, 37, 44, 57, 59, 110, 128-129
Ezzard, William, 13, 27, 96

Fair of 1850, 17
Federal Building, 156
Fillmore, Pres. Millard, 17
Fire of 1917, 125-126
First Baptist Church, 116, 129-130, 153
First Church of Christ, Scientist, 116, 127
First Methodist Church, 34, 50, 63, 93, 97, 115
First National Bank of Atlanta, 156
First Presbyterian Church, 127-128, 153
Five Points, 1, 11, 16, 19, 23, 25, 28, 46, 54, 56, 62, 86, 105, 107, 124, 127, 132, 136, 141, 142, 144, 145, 151, 158, 160, 163, 165
Flatiron Building, 87
Foreacre, Green J., 43, 134
Fourth (now First) National Bank Building, 88
Franklin, William Jasper, 46
Fulton County Centennial parade, 157-158

Garrett, Franklin M., 18, 129, 149
Gate City Guard, 18, 19, 47
Gatins, Joseph F., 113
Gentlemen's Driving Club, 58
Georgia Railroad, 4, 6, 12, 17, 18
Georgian Terrace Hotel, 113, 121, 132, 134, 136, 142
Gilbert, Dr. Joshua, 10
Gilmer, Lt. George R., USA, 2
Goldsmith, J. W., 95
Gone With The Wind, 140-143, 152
Goodrum, James J., 95-96
Goodson, Mrs. Charles, 130
Gordon, Gen. John B., CSA, 59, 62, 63, 83, 84, 89, 97, 124

Governor's Horse Guards, 59, 125
Grady, Henry W., 22, 33, 47-49, 50, 51-52, 56, 59, 62-63, 77, 112, 123, 129
Grady, Mrs. Henry W., 62
Grand Theater, 75-76, 89, 109, 141
Grant, John T., 48, 153
Grant, John W., 53, 98, 120
Grant, William D., 47-48, 92, 98, 149
Gray, James R., 75, 88

Haden, Charles J., 155
Hallman, John C., 35
Hammond, Nathaniel J., 36, 114
Harding, Pres. Warren G., 132
Hardwick, Thomas W., 132
Harris, Jack, 90
Harris, Joel Chandler, 48, 97, 158
Hartsfield, Mayor William B., 142
Haskins, Mrs. C. R., 57
Hayden, Julius, 25
Hayes, Pres. Rutherford B., 37
Healey, Thomas G., 36, 138
Healey Building, 36, 138
Hemphill, William A., 47, 75-76, 78-79, 85, 89, 94
Henry Grady Building, 129
Henry Grady Hotel, 129
Herring, William, 14, 22
High, J. M., 96, 135
High, Mrs. Joseph Madison, 94, 135
High Museum of Art, 135, 143, 157
Hill, Hon. Benjamin H., MC, 31, 50-52, 115
Hill, Rhode, 16, 37, 47, 114, 134
Hood, Lt. Gen. John B., CSA, 22, 23, 25
Hopkins, Charles T., 108
Hopkins, John R., 88-89, 139, 156
Hornady, Mrs. John R., 130-31
Howard, George J., 55
Howard, Troup, 123, 131
Howard, W. P., 26
Howard Theater, 131
Howell, Albert, Jr., 113
Howell, Clark, 13, 94
Howell, Clark, Jr., 76, 120, 132, 133, 138
Howell, Mrs. Clark, Jr., 76, 111
Howell House, 156
Hoyt, Samuel B., 16
Humphries, Elizabeth, 10
Hunnicutt, Calvin W., 15, 54
Hunnicutt and Bellingrath Building, 131

Indians, 1-3
Inman, Edward H., 95
Inman, Mr. and Mrs. Frank M., 122, 155
Inman, Hugh T., 53, 65, 114, 128
Inman, Hugh T., 2nd, 128
Inman, Samuel M., 49, 64-65, 79, 148
Inman, Mrs. Samuel M. (2nd wife), 64, 82, 128, 148
Inman, Shadrach W., 65
Inman, Walker P., 49, 57, 65, 66, 91, 148
Inman, Mrs. Walker P., 94
Inman, Mr. and Mrs. William H., 65-66, 76, 154
International Cotton Exposition, 46-47, 74
Ivy, Hardy, 12, 71, 164

Jackson, Thomas Cobb, 76, 92
Jackson, Mrs. Thomas Cobb (Sarah Grant), 91-92, 118
Jacobs, Dr. Joseph, 54
Jacobs Drug Stores, 54, 109
James, John H., 33-34, 36, 44, 98, 114, 128, 163
Jones, Robert T., Jr. ("Bobby"), 140
Jones, Dr. Willis B., 123, 149
Jordan, Leonidas A., 66-68
Jordon, Mrs. Leonidas A. (Julia Hurt), 66-67. *See also* Little, Mrs. John D.
Joyner, W. R. ("Cap"), 73, 90
Julian, Allen P., 149
Junior League, Atlanta Branch, 151

Kemble, Fanny, 34
Kendrick, Belle, 70-71
Kile, Thomas, 6, 16, 25, 36, 138
Kimball, H. I., 52-53, 57, 64, 134
Kimball House, 36, 38, 53-54, 59, 61, 62, 87, 109
King, George E., 54
King, Porter, 78
King Hardware Co., 54
Kingsberry, Joseph, 58
Kiser, John, 95
Kiser, Marion C., 49-50
Kiser, William H., 91
Knowles, Clarence, 52, 94

Langston, Thomas L., 115
Larendon, C. L., 31
Lawshé, Er, 14, 27, 37, 114

Leide, Enrico, 131
Leyden, Major Austin, 22, 89
Leyden, Mrs. Austin, 22, 89
Leyden house, 14, 22, 57, 89-90, 99, 114, 129, 153, 155
Lindbergh, Charles A., 132-133
Little, John D., 67, 139, 154
Little, Mrs. John D., 67-68, 139, 154
Long, Dr. Crawford W., 13, 54
Long, Stephen H., USA, 4
Longstreet, Lt. Gen. James B., CSA, 51, 79, 83
Lowe, Rebie, 91
Lowe, William B., 91
Lowe, Mrs. William B., 91, 130
Lowry, Col. Robert, 32, 74-75, 94
Lowry, William M., 31-32
Luckie, Alexander F., 6-7, 49
Lumpkin, Gov. Wilson, 3
Lutheran Church of the Redeemer, 143-144
Lyons, Dr. J. Sproyle, 128

McBurney, Edgar Poe, 57, 100, 128, 157
McBurney, Mrs. Edgar Poe (2nd.), 100
McCabe, Mrs. Ellen G., 64, 84, 154
McElreath, Walter, 149
McKinley, Pres. William, 79, 85, 89
McPherson, Gen. James B., U.S.A., 23
Maddox, Robert Flournoy, 32-33, 89
Maddox, Robert Foster, 111
Maher, M. E., 56
Maquino, Antonio, 10-11
Markham, William, 25, 32, 37
Marsh, John R., 141
Marsh, McAllen, 94
Marye, Mrs. P. Thornton, 149
Meador, Thomas H., 76
Memorial Day, 145
Metropolitan Opera in Atlanta, 120-121, 151-152
Mims, Major Livingston, 42-43, 81-82, 84, 95, 113, 129
Mims, Mrs. Livingston, 42-43, 61, 84, 117
Mitchell, Eugene M., 122, 155
Mitchell, Margaret, 122, 140-143, 152
Montgomery's Ferry, 3, 4
Morgan, Thomas H., 155
Murphy, John E., 98-99, 113, 120, 160
Muse, George, 131-32

National Hotel, 28, 30, 76, 88, 126
Neinmeister II (hotel), 76, 115
Newspapers:
Atlanta Constitution, The, 48, 50, 78, 115, 138
Atlanta Daily Intelligencer, 29, 32
Atlanta Herald, 48
Atlanta Journal, The, 45, 49, 76, 77, 86, 91, 118, 124, 125, 128, 131, 132, 133, 136, 140, 141
Georgia Major, The, 44-45
Looking-Glass, The, 77
Masonic Signet, 16
Medical and Literary Weekly, 15
Miscellany, 7-8
Norcross, Jonathan, 5-6, 11-12, 16, 88
Norcross Building, 5, 54, 88
Norris Building, 134
North Avenue Presbyterian Church, 91, 147, 153-154
Nunnally, James H., 106, 123, 155
Nunnally, Mrs. James H., 123
Nunnally's, 106

Opera House, 52-53
Orr, W. W., Doctors' Building, 138
Ottley, John K., 64, 88

Paderewski, Ignace Jan, 89
Paine, Tom, 90
Palmer, Charles F., 138, 155
Patti, Adelina, 80
Paullin, Dr. James E., 147-148
Payne, J. Carroll, 114, 123, 160
Peachtree Arcade, 88, 126
Peachtree Christian Church, 133
Peachtree Towers Apts., 163
Peck, John Calvin, 44
Peck, Willis, 14, 98
Peel, Lucy Cook, 91
Peel, Col. William Lawson, 49, 84, 91, 120, 122, 136, 155
Peel, Mrs. William Lawson, 49, 84, 91, 111, 122, 155
Pemberton, Styth, 55
Perkerson, Medora Field (Mrs. Angus), 141
Pershing Point, 127, 133, 135, 165
Peters, Richard, 12-13, 35, 41, 64, 87, 129-130

Piedmont Driving Club, 52, 72, 103, 110, 112
Piedmont Exposition, 58-59, 78
Piedmont Hotel, 96, 111, 112, 118
Piedmont Park, 78, 83, 85, 110, 117
Pitts, Columbus, 24
Pitts, Tom, 135-136
Polk, Lt. Gen. Leonidas K., CSA, 23
Ponce de Leon Apts., 113, 135, 156
Pope, Maj. Gen. John, USA, 30
Porter, James H., 47, 59, 76, 115
Porter, Mrs. James H., 47, 59-62, 76, 94, 115
Prohibition, 55-56, 108-109

Race riot, 106-108
Ragan, Mrs. James, 134
Ragan, Col. Willis E., 43, 57, 74, 134
Raoul, Eleanor, 119
Raoul, Capt. William Greene, 65, 119, 146
Raoul, Mrs. William Greene, 72
Raoul, William G., Jr., 72-73
Rawson, Mr. and Mrs. William C., 123
Ray, Rev. Anderson, 9
Red Rock Building, 129
Reed, Wallace P., 24-25, 27
Rethberg, Elisabeth, 131
Rhodes, Amos G., 101, 133, 143
Rhodes Center, 143
Rhodes-Haverty Bldg., 134
Rice, Frank P., 20
Richards, Robert H., 44, 58, 70, 114
Richards, Mrs. Robert H. (*See* Mrs. Abbott)
Roosevelt, Pres. Franklin D., 132-133, 137-138, 147-148
Roosevelt, Pres. Theodore, 110, 112
Rose, R. M., 160

St. Luke's Episcopal Church, 23, 116, 153
St. Mark Methodist Church, 116, 153
St. Philip's Episcopal Church (now Cathedral of St. Philip), 87, 116
Salm-Salm, Brig. Gen. Felix, USA, 27
Sawtell, Thomas R., 122, 138, 155
Scott, Frederick M., 154
Seely, Fred L., 98
Sheldon, Dr. Charles A., Jr., 128
Sherman, Gen. William T., USA, 25, 37-38, 116
Shrine convention, 117-118
Shrine Mosque (Fox Theater), 134, 151
Silvey, Drury, 102
Silvey, John, 28-29, 54, 98, 101, 102, 155
Slaton, Gov. John M., 91-92, 118
Slaton, Mrs. John M., 91-92, 118
Smith, Henry H., 72, 103, 113
Smith, Mrs. Henry H., 103
Smith, Gov. Hoke, 104, 106, 111
Smith, Jasper N. ("Uncle Jack"), 69-70, 103-104
Smith, Col. Peter F., 139
Smith, Telamon Cruger Cuyler, 72-74, 103-104
Smith, Mrs. Telamon C. C. (Grace Barton), 103
Southern Commercial Congress, 112
Spalding, Eugene C., 84
Speer, Rev. Eustace W., 9
Speer, William A., 122
Speer, Mrs. William A., 102, 122, 155
Standing Peachtree, 1-2, 4
Steele, A. B., 96
Stephens, Hon. Alexander H., 19, 57, 97, 164

Taft, Hon. William H., Pres.-Elect of US, 111-112
Temple, The, 154
Terry, George W., 11
Thomas, Gen. George H., USA, 22
Thompson, Dr. Joseph, 17, 41, 43, 53, 87
Thompson, Mrs. Joseph, 94
Thornbury's, Miss (school), 80
Thornton, Albert E., 42, 146, 153, 154
Thornton, Mrs. Albert E., 42
Thornton, Mrs. Albert E., Jr., 146
Todd, J. S., 84
Tompkins, Judge Henry B., 67, 154
Toombs, Robert, 31, 67
Traynham, W. L., 113
Trout House (hotel), 17
Trust Company of Georgia, 101
Tutwiler, Charles V., 35

United States Junior Chamber of Commerce, national conventions of, 158-159

Van Winkle, Edward K., 100
Venable, Willis E., 55
Veterans Day, 159
Victoria, Queen of England, memorial service for, 93

Washington Seminary, 102, 123, 124, 141, 156, 161
Werner, Mrs. Louise, 39
Wesley Chapel, 9-10, 20, 21, 23, 27, 34, 116, 128, 163
West, Andrew J., 148
West View Cemetery, 57
Western & Atlantic Railroad, 4, 20
White Hall Tavern, 3, 4, 10
Wight, Ward, 155
Wilkins, Grant, 120
Wilkins, Mrs. Grant, 156
Wilkinson, Mell R., 100, 132, 157
Wilkinson, Mrs. Mell R., 100
William-Oliver Bldg., 138
Williams, Jesse Parker Memorial Hospital, 148
Wilson, Dr. John Stainback, 34-35
Wilson, Woodrow, 47, 112
Wilson Hotel, 131
Wimbish, William A., 98, 130
Winecoff Hotel, 115, 149-150
Winship, Charles R., 128
Winship, George, 41-42, 47, 106, 123, 129, 156
Winship, Joseph, 13, 16, 27, 42, 131
Wood, John N., 39
Wood, Major Gen. Leonard, 124
Woodberry, Miss Rosa, 114, 129, 140
Woods, William B., 38
Woodward, Mayor James, 86, 107
World Baptist Congress, 144-145
WSB, 128
Wylie, Capt. James R., 37, 57, 129

www.ingramcontent.com/pod-product-compliance
Lightning Source LLC
LaVergne TN
LVHW090937080826
845145LV00003B/786

* 9 7 8 0 8 2 0 3 3 4 7 7 6 *